Benign

Grant Robinson

Benign

Copyright ©2021 Grant Robinson

ISBN   978-0-578-33651-0

All rights reserved. No part of this publication may be reproduced, distributed, or transmitted in any form or by any means, including photocopying, recording, or other electronic or mechanical methods, without the prior written permission of the publisher, except in the case of brief quotations embodied in critical reviews and certain other noncommercial uses permitted by copyright law.

Book design by StoriesToTellBooks.com

Benign

Grant Robinson

About the Author

Grant Robinson was born in Watertown, New York, September 19, 1946 at the tip of the wave of baby boomers following World War II. Six years later his parents Stanley and Maretta moved Grant and his siblings Dennis, Kathy, and Maretta to the town of Theresa (which bears a striking resemblance to the Benign, New York, he describes in this book.)

Grant graduated from SUNY at Oswego and earned a master's degree at Michigan State University, married Joan Craner whom he said, "gave me wings," and spent 30 years teaching and amazing students in Swartz Creek, Michigan before retiring in Arizona. Grant and Joan had five daughters Lynn (Paul Hughs) Marks, of Eagle, Idaho, Lori (Jeff) Greenberg of Manhattan Beach, California, Lisa (Thomas, deceased) Robinson of Phoenix, Arizona. They have seven grandchildren grandchildren Steve Marks, Austin and Alyssa Patterson, Chloe and Catherine Greenberg, and Thomas and Tai Van Zant; and three great-grandchildren Brailey, Collin, and Braylon. Grant loved traveling, writing, and making other people laugh.

A lifelong writer, when he was diagnosed with cancer in 1998, Grant began *Windows and Doorknobs*, a series of thoughts and reflections many of them dealing with his hometown. He later decided to write a book that captured his life and times in the mythical town of *Benign* which gave this book its title. Many pieces from *Windows and Doorknobs* appear in *Benign*.

Dear Lynn, Lisa, Lori, and Leann,

The word *explore* comes from the Latin word *explorae* meaning "to cry out." Early explorers often posted lookouts to cry out when land or possible dangers were sighted. Columbus had such lookouts. Columbus also kept two logs of his journey. The first, which he kept secret, was a record of his actual course and distance. The second, a false record of his location, was shared with his crew so they wouldn't be frightened at sailing so far from home. Although I don't yet know all of the directions in which this undertaking may lead, I understand the necessity of exploring beyond the harbor markers.

From my 17th-floor hotel window in Toronto, Canada, I could see the front of the shorter buildings across the street. Each appeared bright and new, presenting passers-by with a shining surface and an inviting promise. However, I could also see the alleys behind those buildings. They were full of unpainted exits, overturned trash, and overloaded dumpsters containing unused resources, missed opportunities, false starts, disappointments, failures, hopes, dreams, and aspirations. Like those dumpsters, this log contains both the by-products of living I've sought to discard in out-of-sight places and the raw materials of new beginnings. However, it contains no false fronts, shining surfaces, or inviting promises. It's simply a search through the dumpsters in the back alleys of my mind.

> Looking at events and circumstances through eyes focused upon possible lessons to be learned has been a life-long obsession. Life has given me many lessons, but seldom in a

logical, systematic pattern. One such lesson is that life is a patient and persistent teacher, willingly repeating a lesson until I've learned it. Or as Al, a good friend, describes it: "The ox is slow, but the Earth is patient." Although this log is an attempt to record those lessons, it isn't always an accurate record of my course, distance, or location. Columbus overestimated his distance by nearly ten percent in his secret log, locating the new world hundreds of miles too far to the west. However, his false log, the one he wrote for others, almost exactly located his discovery.

Note! You may recognize some of the characters, others not, at least not by the names named. That's because I've taken liberties with several of the names and some of the facts. I did so for two important, if not valid, reasons. First, when real names would unnecessarily embarrass someone, I changed them. Second, although at your age it may seem illogical, omitting some facts doesn't necessarily invalidate the truth. Rather, it may help to focus upon the truth more clearly by removing the distractions surrounding it. Let me illustrate with a quotation I love.

> *"Let us begin by committing ourselves to the truth - to see it like it is and tell it like it is - to find the truth, to speak the truth, and to live the truth."*

This quotation expresses a self-imposed goal in my life, more often reached in theory than practice. Although thought isn't responsible for the person thinking it, many of my generation who might agree with the statement would be distracted by the fact it's from Richard M. Nixon's 1968 speech accepting the GOP Presidential Nomination.

My quest to find the truth, to speak it, and to live it explores my first twenty years lived mostly in the small town of Benign, New York twelve miles south of the Canadian border.

I began this log on the summer side of my life and it's been through several stages in my development. I first began writing on small pieces of paper and storing them in desk and dresser drawers. Then I began writing in notebooks. When I didn't have paper and a pencil, I used a small tape recorder. Finally, with the aid of a computer, my left brain attempted a coup. The result is this log. Some of the entries are recent, some go back several years, and many are still drifting in the uncharted waters of my mind. I call this log my *Adversaria*. *Adversaria* is the Latin name for a book used for recording observations, feelings, and notes on anything worth remembering. A sort of "Roam' in" diary, *adversaria* is also the origin of the word adversary. To discover new worlds, you must often be your own adversary. Like Columbus, you must be willing to challenge limitations and confront the unknown. Because our truths may only occasionally intersect, I encourage you to use this log as the seed for your own *Adversaria* by recording your observations, views, feelings, and insights. You can't find truth by following another. To find truth you must follow the truth. That journey begins and ends within you. Here are some suggestions to help you get started.

The secret to setting sail on a sea of ideas isn't in finding the wind but in raising your anchor. Raise your anchor by writing stuff down. Because the only thing more difficult than learning from experience is not learning from experience. Writing about your experiences will generate reflections. Those reflections, each a separate view of yourself, will help you to determine "What's to be learned?" I suspect that's what the expression, "See what you think." means. Besides, if you don't occasionally take time to look at how you're living life, you risk life living you.

So where do you start? Elie Wiesel in *Souls of Fire* has one answer. "The world is so vast, I shall start with the country I know best, my own. But my country is so very large. I had better start with my town. But my town, too, is large. I had best start with my street. No: my home. No: my family. Never mind, I shall start with myself."

There's no incorrect way to write an *adversaria*. Simply select topics or events that reflect your circumstances (current location) and your needs (desired directions). No training, preparation, agenda, or predetermined destination is required. Because writing is translating truth into words, simply connect your pen to your spirit and let your spirit fill the page.

Write what you think rather than what others will think is right. This approach is difficult because knowing what you believe, think, and feel isn't always easy to determine and is often difficult to communicate.

Be willing to write about your defeats as well as your victories. Use your pain as a door leading inward toward greater self-awareness. I agree with **Karen Mal**, *my second favorite singer/song writer after Dylan, when she sings, "My scars are tattoos of the lessons I've learned."*

Read! Reading is one the best ways of getting <u>ready</u> to learn from life's lessons. As you read, take notes on ideas that both reinforce your beliefs and challenge them. Other voices are often useful in helping you to find your own.

My final suggestion is to follow the advice of the great German poet Rainer Maria Rilke who wrote,

> "...have patience with everything unresolved in your heart and try to love the questions themselves as if they were locked rooms or books written in a very foreign language. Don't search for the answers, which could not be given you now, because you would not be able to live them. And the point is, to live everything. Live the questions now. Perhaps then, someday far in the future, you will gradually, without ever noticing it, live your way into the answer..."

A recovering schoolteacher for the last several years, there are days when I look like a tired old man and still others when I feel like one. And although I freely admit I live at the mercy of these stories. They are my best evidence that when it comes to new beginnings, I've had more than a few. These are simple stories, my gift to you; disconnected, disjointed, untidy, some of them are true.

Mandy Aftel wrote, "As you begin to pay attention to your own stories and what they say about you, you will enter into the exciting process of becoming, as you should be, the author of your own life, the creator of your possibilities." Lots of stories, thoughts, and observations were auditioned for this *adversaria*. I hope those selected give you more to chew on than wade through. The majority of it is true, if not factual, and if it didn't happen as I described, it should have. By now you have more questions than answers. Good! That's the way life is supposed to be because our real adventures begin approximately three steps beyond our comfort levels. As you try to figure out a polite response to all of this, please remember that just as there's no wrong way to write an *adversaria*, there's no right way to read one, at least not this one. You may read it from start to stop, backward, from the center outward, or not at all. All are equally valid responses because, although it's written to you, I didn't write it for you.

Love,

Dad

Introduction

I recently read about an experiment by a French naturalist, Jean-Henri Fabre, who placed a row of Processionary Caterpillars around the top of a flowerpot, one behind the other, in an unbroken chain. Processionary Caterpillars move through pine trees in long processions with their heads tightly pressed against the rear of the one in front of it. Although he expected them to get tired, hungry, and eventually disperse to look for food, the caterpillars continued following each other around in a circle. They died a few days later of starvation within sight of food.

Sadly, far too many people live processionary lives. They blindly follow others because of habit or tradition or fear or for money or they're following orders or because they mistake activity for accomplishment. They live and die within sight of everything they need for a happy and rewarding life because they can't leave the circle of security they lean upon. Because such well-worn paths seldom lead inward or outward, they remain in orbit until they're exhausted and beaten. Perhaps that's why they're called "beaten paths."

I was born September 19, 1946, sharing a natal year with 3.5 million others who represented the vanguard of the Baby Boom Generation. Boomers have never been much for beaten paths. They are known for leaving the circle to seek an alternative reality.

The ancient Romans would call me *Laudator temporis acti* (a praiser of time past) and say this book is about events *consule planco*, their equivalent for "in the good old days." For me, this undertaking is also what Native Americans call a Vision Quest. Each chapter is a composite of snapshots locked in time. As my laptop became my mind's tongue, I realized my most life-influencing events were what Virginia Woolf called, "moments of being."

Although frayed from repeating, it is not my intent to retouch these tattered stories in an attempt to leave them better than I found them. However, while reality goes naked, memories are clothed in needs, hopes, and values. Memories are selective, fragmented, filtered by self-esteem, and edited by ego. Therefore, I am left with unfinished reconstructions that continue to change with time. For a while, I thought I understood the wisdom of Julia Cameron's observation that "The way we describe our lives and understand them is ultimately and inextricably connected to the way we live them." Now I realize I have no idea what in the hell that means. Thus, I've learned not to use a quote that's smarter than I am.

Caution! This book isn't the product of a balanced life or a focused intellect. Rather than beginning, it just starts. It doesn't have an ending; it just stops. It doesn't have a plot (against anyone), but you'll meet plenty of characters, including family, friends, dreamers, drifters, life-living lovers, life-loving givers, takers, prophets, pilgrims, poets, pillars, preachers, and parts of yourselves. It doesn't follow a logical sequence of events because my life isn't a seamless garment. Rather, it's worn and torn from use, abuse, and the daily grind of living. But it's the only garment I have and this book reflects those sacred moments of my journey when I wrapped myself in it like a man seeking comfort from a storm.

Although the world is full of books of deep thoughts, deep meanings, and incredible insights, this is not one of them. Rather, it's a baby boomer's journey through my times of yore. Albert Einstein said, "The release of atom power has changed everything except our way of thinking." Looking back from a hilltop in the here-and-now, it's exciting to see just how far my generation of baby boomers has come, how much we've changed our way of thinking, and how much we changed the world. Boomers came of age in the Sixties during Kennedy's *New Frontier*. For many of us, Hal Borland's words, "A frontier is never a place; it is a time and a way of life," are an accurate description of our *Wonder Years*. That's also true of the way of life in Benign, my hometown in upstate New York, for it was more than a town; it was a time.

Feeling like echoes wrapped in shadows, my memories of growing up a boomer in Benign often summon me home like my mother's call to supper. Running and laughing, I let the screen door slam behind me as I seek the embrace of warmth lost. This book is about the events, places, and people that still beat within the hearts of baby boomers. These snapshots are offered as evidence that the future can grow in the shadow of the past.

Chapter One

The Begots and Bygones of 1946

Benign Was More Than a Town; It Was a Time

William Pete asked, "Can one desire too much of a good thing?" More than a bad case of nostalgia, those coming of age in the '50s and '60s now know just how much of a good thing they once had. That's especially true for the citizens of Benign where everyone knew everybody's pedigree. Benign was more than a town; it was a time when parents taught their children that everyone was special, but no one was more special. "Get down off your high horse", "Don't act so high and mighty", "Don't be looking down your nose", and "I'll bring you down a peg," were expressions commonly uttered by the parents of Benign. It was a time when humbleness was drummed into children until they got it through their heads. Benign, like every small town, had a handful of muckety-mucks with enough money or community status to act hoity-toity, but their closet skeletons were well enough known to prevent them from flying much higher than everyone else.

Benign was a time when Hopalong Cassidy's Creed instructed children to obey their parents, respect others, show good manners, practice thrift, and that, "The highest badge of honor a person can wear is honesty." It was a time when Roy Rogers Riders Rules taught children to protect the weak, study hard, be kind to animals, respect the flag, love America, and never waste food.

Benign was a time when policemen walked a beat, movies had both a main and a second feature, libraries had a Reader's Guide to Periodical Literature, we used a penny for a fuse, we hung icicles on the Christmas tree, school desks had a hole where the missing inkwell went, women's jeans had the zipper on the side, and on special occasions, your mother made Jell-o Salad with mandarin oranges, miniature marshmallows, walnuts, and Miracle Whip. Benign was more than a town, it was Ovaltine, Old Spice Aftershave, Mrs. Well's Tomato Ketchup, White House coffee, malt shops, poodle shirts, Mrs. Paul's Fish Sticks, the Dead-End Kids, bubble Christmas lights, dish towels in laundry detergent, Marshmallow Peeps, *MAD Magazine*, and *You Were There* with Walter Cronkite.

The Same Small-Town Inside of Us

Once you know the truth, you cannot go back to not knowing. Living the truth that you know is the greatest service you can offer the world.

~Iyanla Vanzant

Already in a rotten mood, turning down a wrong street only validated his current temperament. Mumbling his disgust, Grant was in the middle of an illegal U-turn when he saw it. There, gleaming in the Tucson sun stood an oasis, a shining sanctuary, and a basilica in the Sonoran Desert. The Five and Diner wasn't just a diner, but a safe harbor from Grant's self-imposed storm.

As he entered the front portal, Grant was transported back into the sparkling stainless-steel paradise of his teens. Each booth had a "two plays for a quarter" Wurlitzer jukebox and, as he slid across the shiny, red vinyl seat, Grant could taste the cholesterol-enhanced air. Taking a deep breath of nostalgia, he rejoiced at again being in a world without pretense, where everything tasted fried, where there were no tofu or "heart smart" items on the menu, and where everything came with wet (gravy covered) fries. With a smile reminding him of a rainbow, Shannon took Grant's order (a chocolate milk shake, a cheeseburger, and fries), as his body began absorbing the beat of "Mustang Sally," the first of a dollar's worth of plays.

Grant's mood continued to mellow as "Stagger Lee" and "Woolly Bully" bathed him in high school memories of the class of '64. There had been ninety-eight graduates and Grant wondered, not about how many were still alive, but about how many of his former classmates were living lives that were still on fire. No doubt weathered by life forces, how many of those smiling faces still held the glow of joy-filled eyes? How many had fulfilled the promise of their youth? In a diner fifty years from the auditorium where they had received their ribbon-wrapped admission tickets to their futures, Grant wondered how many were still searching and how many had traded their wings for luggage.

Grant left high school to explore a world where nothing seemed impossible, where rivers, mountains, and deserts were challenges to be met, and where his search was focused outward. Now the world surrounding his diner-encased wonderings seemed dangerous, where rivers, mountains, and deserts were often obstacles generating doubt and where his search had turned inward as he brailles feelings he cannot see.

Grant was once a young man who was, as they say, ten feet tall and bulletproof. He was idealistic, cocky, indestructible, and never drew a blurred line. Although Grant knew, in theory, he could be wrong about something; in practice, he knew it was extremely unlikely. However, that was before life classified, scrutinized, traumatized, neutralized, sanitized, analyzed, categorized, and conventionalized him. It was before he was encapsulated, exposed, deposed, deceived, denied, robbed, ridiculed, cheated, mistreated, displaced, defined, confined, neglected, and rejected. Now he is an aging boomer on the front edge of a monster wave threatening to swamp Social Security.

A recovering schoolteacher for the last several years, there are days when Grant looks and feels like a tired old man. Now retired, Grant begins each day in the morning shadows of Arizona's Catalina Mountains with a light breakfast and a handful of pills from a blue plastic box with seven compartments, each labeled for a day of the week. Now, not only is the President and most members of Congress younger than he is, Grant is older than almost everyone with any influence or authority over him, from police officers to his minister. Grant has underwear older than his doctor, strangers call him Pops, and his grandkids belong to a generation of soft talking mumblers.

Perhaps the best thoughts have already been thought; at least that is what T.N. suspects. Off-again-on-again friends since boyhood, T.N. and Grant grew up in the same small town, knew the same people, attended the same high school and dated the same girls. Their friendship began under watchful eyes as they learned to say their ABCs, fear polio, pledge the flag, ride two-wheelers, and feel guilty about starving children in China. After high school, Grant went off to college carrying a bag of unanswered questions in search of something he couldn't name. T.N. also went to college seeking answers, but to different questions in search of a different reality. While Grant searched outside himself as an education major, T.N.'s search turned inward majored in psychology.

A weaver of dreams with rattlesnake wit, T.N. had a troubadour's heart in the eye of his own hurricane. He was a gazer of stars who valued silence, nurtured friendships, and was just as interested in what people felt as in what they thought. Although he enjoyed people, many of his best friends were books. Once, in a thank you note for a book Grant had given him, he wrote, "Books not only make good friends, they make good friends better."

Nestled on the banks of the Indian River twelve miles south of the U.S. - Canadian border in Upstate New York, their town of Benign, nicknamed "The Nicest Place You'll Ever Find," was the core of their world. With a population of less than a thousand, Grant and T.N. grew up bathed in the innocence of the fifties. Back then, everyone they knew was still alive, they believed in wishes made on stars or while blowing out birthday candles, they hated afternoon naps, and they had yet to feel the pain of a brokenhearted love. Back then, houses had front porches that served as the center of their neighborhood's social life. Each evening, neighbors gathered on them to chat, drink fresh-squeezed lemonade, and, on someone's birthday, enjoy homemade ice cream. Benignians looked out for each other, and those evenings united them, gave them a sense of belonging, and provided them with a sense of community. To Grant, they were what Julia Cameron calls a "soul clan."

Growing up, Grant's family not only didn't lock their doors, but they also couldn't remember the last time anyone had seen the keys. baby boomers like Grant and T.N. were raised in simpler times. They lived in *Leave It To Beaver* mentalities with *Mayberry* moralities. Everyone knew everyone as the textures of their lives were woven around the lives of their fellow Benignians. Grant lost that sense of oneness after moving away, only to find it again when he began living life on Tucson time, sixty years and three thousand miles downstream from where he was spawned.

Grant knows almost nothing of T.N.'s ancestral heritage, except that T.N.'s grandfather emigrated illegally from Ontario, Canada to Northern New York at the age of nineteen by walking across the frozen St. Lawrence River. He married young and inhabited a farmer's life for the remainder of his eighty years. After college, while Grant was off changing the world on his own, T.N. returned to Benign to invest the same forty years in small-town living with Arlo, his dog, and a full-time woman he nicknamed

Crescendo. Crescendo, (Cathy) is the daughter of Max and Roslyn Bartlett who operated the now-defunct milk and cheese plant out on the Red River Road. The only evidence of the plant still surviving the 1996 fire is part of one stonewall and a faded road sign reading, "Our Cheese Is Old Enough to Vote and Sharp Enough to Kill a Rat."

Until a few months ago, the last several years passed between T.N. and Grant unused. When he was a teenager, Grant could not wait to leave Benign. Then, following his retirement, Grant began visiting Benign in the quiet places within him. Because we are bound to others by the befores and afters we've shared and because they were the only people left in Grant's life (except for his brother) who remembered him as a kid, Grant first wrote T.N.. Then, a few days later, he wrote Cindy, a former high school sweetheart he nicknamed "Brink" and still owned and operated what Grant calls an, unlike mind.

Seeking a deeper connection to his roots, Grant began writing and sending T.N. some stories about the life lessons he had learned during their shared childhoods, asking him if he would respond with his thoughts and insights. T.N. replied with a ten-word e-mail stating, "I can only show you what you're willing to reveal." With that single sentence, they began what has become a steady exchange of curiosity. It was a simple formula; Grant sent T.N. his image and T.N. sent back his reflection. Two days after TN's initial response, Grant received a second e-mail.

Salutations Grant,

> What has it been, ten years or more? Regardless, I rejoiced at hearing from you again. Some time back I'd heard you'd retired, but didn't know you were currently residing at

Rancho Relaxo, sucking up the sunshine as a non-indigenous Arizonan in the land of rattlesnakes and pokey plants.

Just as police have badges and guns, judges have black robes and wooden gavels, chefs have big spoons and even bigger white hats, priests have collars and crucifixes, and generals have stars, bars. and scars, when you were a teacher you had a red pencil and a big desk to symbolize your authority. Now that you are using a pen to fill some of the life-spaces generated by your retirement, what symbolizes your authority as a writer?

Do you remember Teddy Hover? He was a grade behind us and lived with his grandmother in the old stone McAllister house adjacent to Decker's Laundromat. Not much brighter than when the two of you played "chicken foot" with jackknives on the playground, he has been our town sheriff since he inherited the job from his father nearly ten years ago. I think the only reason he became sheriff was to play with the siren and to have a decent car to drive instead of his timeworn Ford.

Until recently, none of us thought much about Teddy's job performance. We were content because, if you live in Benign and he caught you speeding, he generally let you go with a warning. One afternoon last summer, Teddy was off fishing on Black Lake when a man robbed the Texaco out on Route 37. The robbery went badly, and the robber ended up barricaded inside. Someone must have called Teddy's cell phone because within minutes he came tearing up 37, his Econoline shuddering under the strain. As he approached the gas station he could see several officers, guns drawn, crouched behind their police cars. The deputies were relieved when they saw Teddy steaming toward them. However, their delight turned to amazement and then to alarm when Teddy roared past them and, without slowing down, crashed into the front of the gas station. Still in shock, the officers then watched Teddy jump out of his car unhurt and take the stunned robber into custody.

The newspaper and television coverage of the daring capture brought mixed reviews from our barbershop conservatives and the Chat-A-Wyle Diner liberals. Some thought he was courageous and dedicated while others thought his response was foolhardy and reckless. However, all agreed Teddy was a bold, brave, hard-luck hero who had acted with the best of intentions. To show the town's appreciation and support, we held a big celebration, including a parade and a concert by the Indian River Central High School Marching Band. We also put donation jars in Gabriel's Bakery and other town businesses to pay for the repairs to Teddy's car. Following the parade, our new mayor in front of the entire town presented him with a check. When asked what he planned to do with the money, Teddy replied, "I appreciate you getting all the dents out of my car and for the new paint job. I had planned on getting rid of it, but now that it looks so nice, I'm going to keep it and use your check to get the brakes fixed."

As with Teddy, too often a person's behavior reveals only what we're expecting to see. I hope to avoid doing the same as I respond to the stories you send me because, although you and I see the same sun, moon, stars, and sky, we've always seen different horizons. Therefore, I'm going to Target or Wal-Mart and purchase a crap detector. I'm getting one of the more expensive shockproof, water-resistant models that can differentiate between style and substance, radiating and reflecting, interesting and relevant, curiosity and suspicion, and between the menu and the meal.

You wrote that you wanted to, "wring the truth out of the stories of our formative years in search of what's to be learned?" I submit, Grant, that it is not possible to know the truth and not speak it. Truth has many doors and, as a writer, you are called to seek and then speak yours. By doing so, you'll provide both windows and doorknobs for fellow seekers. We are all on open-ended soul journeys seeking truth. Truth requires seeking because it cannot reveal itself any more than a hammer can hit itself; a tooth can bite itself, scissors can cut themselves, or a microscope can magnify itself.

Let me again say how pleased I was to hear from you and how delighted I am with your offer to share your writings with me. That said, I recommend you consider Herman Demian's observation that "Nothing in the world is more distasteful to a man than to take the path that leads to himself."

Knowing you as well as I do, let me answer what I know will be your question of "What is Truth?" Truth can be heard, but we seldom hear it. It can be seen, but we seldom recognize it. It can be spoken, but frequently it's disguised by what we say. To the thirsty, it's a drink of water. To the hungry, it's a loaf of bread. It's what's left after everything that isn't in our best interest is taken away and, when we die, it's all we take with us. It's different for each of us, yet we all have it in common.

T.N.

PS: Your images of Benign no longer exist outside your memories. Countless cul-de-sacs have extended the old neighborhoods into what was once surrounding farmland. Regardless of their design, these newer homes lack the front porches of our generation. Today we have shrub-encased patios and instead of talking, sharing, and belonging, we remain isolated and alone. Sadly, we have neighbor-less neighborhoods and despite what the billboard out on the interstate says, I fear we are no longer the nicest place you'll ever find.

Heroes, Lovers, Loners, Losers, And Whacked Out Weirdoes

Salutations Grant,

Greetings from Benign, currently a subarctic pimple on the frozen backside of heck. (My ten-day-old New Year's Resolution is to clean up my language.) After sixty of these darn winters, I'm hoping to get used to them soon. However, complaints aside, I love winter. Like gravity, you can trust winter because it's clean, sharp-edged real, and uncompromisingly consistent. Winter is Mother Nature's way of teaching us that she and Father Time are older, stronger, and wiser than we mortals. They never lose an argument, are not sensitive to my longings and strivings, and aren't judgmental of my failures and shortcomings. Just as bread rises at its own speed and flowers blossom within their own time, winter comes without malice or apologies on its own terms and timetable, content to leave me wrapped in my own weavings.

Yes, you are still very much invited and we look forward to seeing you in March. However, in case sun-soaked Arizona has erased it from your memory, March blizzards are common. Therefore, you might want to consider bringing a warm coat to defeat the wintery chills. Muddy and mucky, March is my least favorite month, right behind November, February, or perhaps the dog days of August. (My second resolution is to be more decisive.)

Comfortably cocooned in front of a roaring wood fire, I spent the evening enjoying your recollections of our elementary school adventures. Now, between adding additional logs, I'll catch you up on the comings and goings of each of those you mentioned. Miss Dabb, our fourth-grade teacher, was still a Miss when she died at age seventy-three in a Watertown hospital, back when we said people died of old age. Mr. Fields, our elementary school principal, enjoyed nearly thirty years of retirement before he also graduated from life. You will be pleased to know that, like a side of beef from Jerry Frost's Meat Mart, Mr. Fields aged into tenderness. His harshness softened by time, he and his wife were often seen walking hand-in-hand by the river in Veterans Park.

You'll never guess who just began his second term as our mayor. Give up? It was Tinker! Can you believe our gene pool-challenged, pharmacological-dependent, boyhood buddy, who pursued a high school education for five years without catching it, would one day become Mayor? Although he had a random-access memory long before any computer (He thinks Pearl Harbor was a black singer and Magenta is a stripper.), Tinker is now Benign's first citizen, spending his days strutting (with a distinct heterosexual purpose) around town smoking El Producto cigars.

Of his first five years following high school, Tinker, a man with convictions, served four in the Navy and one in a Florida jail. Although the reasons for his incarceration were forever sealed as part of a plea agreement, there are rumors he was arrested for trying to sell a Methodist Church to a land developer who sought to replace it with a parking lot. Then, acting as his own attorney, he pleaded diminished capacity because he said the high-power electrical lines adjacent to his apartment distorted the magnetic fields in his brain. These rumors may or may not be true, but those of us who know Tinker also know how far his tongue can stretch the truth.

Upon his release, Tinker returned to Benign to continue a life of douchebaggery while serving the next two years as a short-order cook and utensil sanitizer at The Second Chance Diner until, under the influence, he cut off two fingertips trying to open an eight-pound (restaurant size) can of Heresy Chocolate Syrup with a hatchet. He then worked at the Miller's Brewery near Syracuse until he moved back to town to open a hardware store called Whatchamajiggers in the old train depot building. Five years later, with his hardware business a huge success, he began opening more stores around Upstate New York. Two years ago, with his innate ability to turn bullshit into buttermilk still intact, he purchased Bicklehop's New and Used Cars and changed the name to Deals on Wheels. That's when Benignians began repeating the phrase, "Tinker is to integrity as Liberace is to boxing."

While working at The Second Chance, Tinker met and married Tanawanda Joe, a badass trucker chick who was reported to have laid everything but the Atlantic Cable. A college graduate turned rebel with a master's degree in foreign languages in her back pocket, Tanawanda spoke six languages and never said no in any of them. By the time she was twenty-five years old, restraint was the only thing she hadn't tried. However, to her credit, after being saved in soup kitchens in Cheyenne, Fort Worth, and Albuquerque, she settled down to be a faithful, loving wife and a great mother.

Tanawanda and Tinker seemed happy enough until about a year ago. After giving him at least a dozen second chances, she attacked him in his sleep by trying to amputate his "manly stalwartness" with a Ronco Vegetable Peeler. Although the details of the assault have been forever sealed as part of the divorce settlement, everyone knows the attack was retribution for his repeated extramarital "tinkering." As you can imagine, the entire episode was a major scandal in our small berg for months. Gynocentric Tinker, however, took the divorce in stride saying, "They say nearly half of all marriages end in divorce. That sounds terrible until you realize the other half ended in death. I'd say I lucked out."

With you living out of state and out of touch for so long, I'm sorry to have to share some very sad news. Lost and alone on streets not so benign, Graham came home a hero from Vietnam in 1972 with a limp, a battered spirit, a purple heart, and a life wrapped in pain he couldn't unravel.

Graham worked part-time jobs when his demons allowed it, filling his last years with sad luck days. His first and best job was at Squealer Feeds until most of it burned in an electrical storm. In blinding heat, he lost both his job and address as firefighters lost their fight to save his back-room home. With a heart full of emptiness and eyes too full of memories to focus on much of anything, Graham began drifting in and out of odd jobs in search of something to do with a life devoid of meaning. Eventually, he turned to the bottle to forget a past life he'd never find again. Liking his wine dry and his whiskey rye, Graham couldn't find a bar he didn't like. Over time, as he began filling his dark world with neon-lighted places, his friends peeled away to be replaced by strangers with lonely faces. Ending most weekends as a passed-out barroom brawler, Graham no longer put up any resistance to what life had to offer as he joined the ranks of the nameless homeless. I remember once he asked me, "Why does my country hate and resent me for going where it sent me?"

With her features feather-soft against his memory, the only way Graham could see her was to close his eyes. Two months married; they were living lives on fire for each other when her light was snuffed out in the blinding flash of a bombing raid on her Vietnamese village. Graham didn't talk about her often, but there wasn't a day he wouldn't have willingly traded all of his tomorrows for a single day with her in it.

The last time I saw Graham he was wearing his misfortunes as lightly as his smile, asking tourists for sidewalk handouts. With his future as faded as his jeans, everyone turned away from the haunting image of him trading his pride for loose change. It was the first time I had seen him sober in months and we enjoyed several minutes of reminiscing about childhood innocence. Later, with a hand feeling like leather, he grasped mine in appreciation for the folding money. Then, before hurrying off, he said, "There are some storms, T.N., that can't be weathered." Three days later, convinced his life was little more than a bad trip, Graham took one last ride. Never taking his foot off the gas, witnesses said he was shifting gears and smiling when he crashed his motorcycle into paradise. With days too hard to get through, dying was just one last thing to do.

Moose, known for winning the Firemen's Labor Day Kitchen Sink Throwing Contest six years running (a Benign record), married young and died young, just four years ago. At fifty-eight, he became a colon cancer statistic, leaving behind a wife, three daughters, and a growing number of grandchildren. We laughed at the funeral when his brother told a story about Moose camouflaging his pickup during deer hunting season. Then, near dark on the first day out, he had to walk two miles to a farmhouse because he couldn't find his truck. I miss Moose for several reasons, but mostly because his thoughts came to you factory direct.

Although we are still a water-tank tower one-traffic light town with our share of loners, losers, whacked-out weirdoes, and ex-con con artists, we are also home to lovers, poets, visionaries, and unsung heroes. We are looking forward to your visit. I'm especially looking forward to again breaking bread with you at the diner. It's a long story, but the Chat-A-Wyle is now called The Second Chance and yes, the burgers are as good as ever.

T.N.

"Richard Nixon Is a No Good, Lying Bastard."
~Harry S Truman

Harry S Truman, the last American President not to attend college, was Stanley Robinson's favorite President long before June 9, 1975, when a *Time Magazine* article quoted Truman as having said, "I never did give anybody hell. I just told the truth and they thought it was hell." As one of four Division Heads at the St. Regis Paper Company in Deferiet, New York, Stanley, Grant's father, supervised over three hundred employees in the Cutter Room. Truman's seventeen-word quote perfectly described Stanley's management style, a mixture of a strong work ethic, a Roman candle temper, and an incredibly low tolerance for bullshit.

Just twelve minutes into the 262nd day of 1946, Grant Noble Robinson joined the 1.4 million baby boomers beginning their life that year. The life expectancy in 1946 was 63, the average house cost $5,600, the average income was $2,500, gas cost 15 cents a gallon, and a letter could be sent anywhere in the United States for 3 cents. If you entered a grocery store with $1.50, you could leave with a dozen eggs, a loaf of bread, a gallon of milk, and 48 cents in change. The Slinky, made from 80 feet of wire, was introduced to toy shelves, W. C. Fields died, and Paul Harvey began telling *The Rest of the Story*. The groundhog saw its shadow at 7:52 AM, the United Nations held its first meeting, Dr. Spock published *The Common Sense Book of Baby and Child Care* that would revolutionize parenting, and Harry S Truman, who said, "Richard Nixon is a no good, lying bastard. He can lie out of both sides of his mouth at the same time, and if he ever caught himself telling the truth, he'd lie just to keep his hand in," was the thirty-third President of the United States.

That same week, in the same hospital, Tnarg Nosnibor (nicknamed T.N.) entered life to become one of Grant's lifelong friends. Three months earlier, Tom and Tina Alexander gave life to Graham, who'd join Grant and T.N. as the third musketeer. Grant, T.N., and Graham were destined to play major roles in each other's development. Living within two blocks of each other, they'd have the same teachers, play on the same ball diamonds, share homework answers, attend the same school dances, and go woodchuck, duck, and deer hunting together. Their friendship would survive the typical childhood squabbles, disagreements over who'd win the World Series, the competition for the affection of the same girls, and arguing over whether Kennedy or Nixon should be president. Graham's full name was Graham Edward Alexander, but his sixth-grade classmates nicknamed him "Crackers" after Graham Crackers. And despite Graham losing his new bride in a bombing raid in a far-off place called the Mekong Delta, their three-way friendship would survive T.N. supporting the Vietnam Conflict, Grant protesting it, and Graham fighting it.

Just Something Tinker Did

If I didn't talk in my sleep, I'd still be married.

~Tinker

By the end of 1954, anyone owning a television knew that M&M's were the new chocolate-covered peanut candies that melted in your mouth, not in your hand. That same year, Air Force One became the official name of the president's plane, and *Sports Illustrated* and Tolkien's *Lord of the Rings* were published. Elvis released his first record, "That's All Right," and the Nautilus, the first nuclear-powered submarine, was launched. And on Tuesday, September 7, 1954, Grant met Brewster Slater on their first day of third grade.

The day before, on Labor Day, the Slater family moved into the old Edward's house on Morgan Street, just around the corner from Grant's front door. When Brewster told Grant, T.N., and Crackers that his nickname was Tinker, they agreed Tinker was a better moniker than Brewster. Tinker had a mineral companion, his best friend, thirty years before pet rocks became popular. None of the Musketeers knew how he got the nickname Tinker or where Tinker got his rock. Those weren't the only mysteries surrounding Tinker. They didn't know where he lived before he came to Benign or why he always threw his sack lunch over the fence to Old Lady Huddleston's dog every morning on his way to school. Nor did they know why Tinker always climbed in and out through his woodshed window instead of using the door. They didn't think much about Tinker's odd habits and accepted them as just something Tinker did.

Every morning, rain, shine, or snow, Tinker and his baseball-sized rock walked Grant to school. As they walked, Tinker would kick his rock a few feet ahead and, when they caught up, he'd kick it again. At school, Tinker hid his rock in the bushes near the side door and then, after school, he'd kick it home. Tinker was very attached to his rock and kept and kicked the same one throughout their elementary school years. Grant never saw Tinker without it, including after school, on weekends, or during summer vacations. It wasn't until they got older that Tinker's relationship with his rock interfered with his relationship with his friends, especially Grant. Because he'd seldom carry it, they grew tired of waiting for him. Kicking his rock when they went to someone's house to play or down to Clock's store for candy or on their way to the school slowed them down. After a while, Tinker stopped catching up as he went his own way. Grant didn't understand why Tinker preferred his rock to his friends; it was just something Tinker did. However, Grant came to understand that as we grow older, we may outgrow some of the relationships that sustained our growth. Unfortunately, Tinker grew up to be a no-can-do kind of guy whose silver tongue spoke fluent bullshit.

Caput Mundi (Capital of the World)

Conformity is the death of the soul.

~Adli Stevenson

Friday, August 8, 1952 – Grant's Family Become Benignians

In 1952, there were two Benigns. The first is the old guard consisting of Republican farmers and the status quoers living in town. Far fewer now than in the '50s and '60s, this group still controls Benignian politics, including the town government, school board, and the various service groups. Native Benignians say George Washington once visited Benign, but there is no mention of it in any of his writings. They also say Jimmy Carter visited Benign during his first bid for the Presidency. Again, there is no written record of such a visit. However, a picture of candidate Bill Clinton eating a Big Mac in a McDonalds twenty miles away in Watertown captured the front page of the *Watertown Daily Times*.

The second Benign, according to the residents of nearby villages, is a village full of cranks, crackpots, eccentrics, oddballs, and a substantial number of nonconformists. Benignians don't mind such characterizations. Just the opposite, they not only feel they add to Benign's charm and quaintness. They also help bring in more summer tourists' dollars. Over the years, Benign has attracted several artists who, by the nature of how artists think, readily supply what the tourists expect from an artist community.

Although Benignians often say they have an abundance of the "terminally weird" living in town, that's strictly for tourist consumption. In truth, Benignians believe they live in the epicenter of truth and sanity while a crazy world revolves around them. Such a belief isn't unusual for New

Yorkers. It's no secret that New Yorkers believe they are superior to everyone else, especially Texans who claim the same superiority. After all, New York is the Empire State.

Five-year-old Grant wasn't happy about moving to Benign. The only home he'd known was the upstairs apartment over his grandparents at 666 Davison Street in Watertown. Grant was too young to notice the tension between his parents and his grandmother turning into an all-out war. All he knew was that he missed being able to use the back stairs to visit his grandma's always-full teddy bear cookie jar. Although Dennis, Grant's younger brother, couldn't remember ever living in the upstairs apartment, having regularly attended Sunday school, he understood the meaning of 666 and worried that being conceived at that address meant he'd surely go to hell. That fear was reinforced when he realized Dennis spelled backward is sinned.

The oldest people in Grant's world were his grandparents. However, it wasn't until he read a book in the sixth grade about the Arizona Rangers that he gained some measure of perspective on their ages. Both born in 1895, Noble and Lena were only six years old when the Arizona Rangers was formed. Before seeking Statehood, just 26 Rangers were given the task of ridding the entire Arizona Territory of outlaws and cattle rustlers. Grant thought it was cool that his grandparents were alive back in the real Wild West days of gunfighters, outlaws, and Indian wars. Grant was again impressed by his grandparents' ages when, in his 10th grade American History Class, he learned that, in addition to Alaska and Hawaii in 1959, they were also alive when Utah in 1896, Oklahoma in 1907, and New Mexico and Arizona in 1912, were admitted to the Union.

Noble lived a solitary life for most of his 83 years. Grant seldom caught his grandfather in a smile, and when he did, it meant Noble was talking about horses. Noble disliked tractors, preferring a good team of horses "any damn day of the week." Following the Crash of 1929, Noble left the farm during the Great Depression to make a living as a lumberjack, mailing money home to his family. The Great Depression taught Noble to avoid spending money like most people avoid root canals. It also taught him to distrust banks, Wall Street, and the government except for the man they considered the savior of the country, Franklin D. Roosevelt. In nearly every conversation, he'd say, "The country is going to hell in a handbasket, but I don't figure on living all that much longer, so it don't much matter to me."

Noble-isms

The Great Depression my ass. In the name of sweet Jesus, I'd like someone to explain to me just what the hell was so great about it.

Prohibition lasted from 1920 until 1933, during which I lived entirely on food and water.

Heathens beget heathens and politicians beget taxes.

Pickpockets steal your money and run. Politicians do just the opposite.

The Black Sambo Incident

A man convinced against his will is not convinced.

~Laurence J. Peter

In 1951, J.D. Salinger, published *Catcher in the Rye*, Herman Woulk published *Caine Mutiny*, Disney released *Alice in Wonderland*, and the cult classic *The Day the Earth Stood Still* debuted. That same year, President Truman fired General Douglas MacArthur, Swanson introduced Turkey Pot Pies, Chrysler introduced power steering, and Grant played the part of Tommy Turnip in his kindergarten's Parade of Vegetables. In 1951, Congress ratified the Twenty-second Amendment, limiting presidents to two terms, Americans were introduced to Tupperware, the Topps Company issued its first baseball card series, and on Tuesday, September 3, 1951, Grant began his first year of school at the Cooper Street School in Watertown, New York. Of that year, Grant remembers his frequent trips to the corner to sit on a piano stool. Another of Grant's kindergarten memories is of a confrontation with Nancy, a classmate. When she tried taking a puzzle away from him, the tussle ended with her in tears when Grant hit her over the head with the heavy, wooden Little Black Sambo puzzle. According to family legend, Grant felt no remorse for what his family came to call the Black Sambo Incident. Labeled immature for his age and unable to get along with others, Grant's kindergarten teacher wouldn't promote him to the first grade. When informed Grant would have to repeat kindergarten, Stanley exclaimed, "How in the hell does anyone flunk kindergarten?"

As fate would have it, a month later, Stanley moved his family to Benign, a small, sleepy, slow-paced Mayberry kind of town, twenty-six miles away. The move gave Grant a fresh start in school; Benign didn't have a kindergarten so Grant went to the first grade by default. However, because Grant believed his actions were justified, the resulting punishment of having to eat his morning graham crackers on a piano stool in the corner caused an early and lasting suspicion of both teachers and rules, teaching him there's nothing poetic about justice. He would later learn that in all conflicts, violence is always an option, seldom an answer, never a solution and that beating others over the head with his truth may silence others, but seldom converts them.

Footnote

Helen Bannerman's original story was about a boy in India, which explains the tigers. Sambo became an African American boy when the story reached the United States. As early as the Civil War the name Sambo, as it was in India, became a derogatory, racist stereotype.

Saturday, March 25, 2006 - The Second Chance

As he entered the diner for the first time in nearly thirty years, the sights, smells, and memories of his teenage years overwhelmed Grant's senses. Now a stranger, he could feel the weight of small-town eyes following him across the room.

Sitting across from each other in Grant's once-favorite booth, T.N. asked, "What in heaven's name brought you to Casablanca?"

It took Grant a few seconds before he remembered and replied, "My health. I came to Casablanca for the waters."

"The waters? What waters? We're in the desert," T.N. said with a wide grin.

"I was misinformed," Grant said before they both began laughing.

"I wondered if you'd remember."

"I might not have had I not watched it again a couple of weeks ago. It's still one of my favorite movies," Grant told him.

"Yeah, mine too," T.N. said as he dropped a quarter into the slot and pushed B14 on the small Wurlitzer jukebox on the wall in their booth. Almost immediately, they heard Don McLean's voice filling the diner.

"Good selection," Grant grinned as he opened a menu. "'American Pie' is a great song."

"Yeah. Not only does McLean pay tribute to the rock n' roll songs of our glory days, but he also pays tribute to Buddy Holly, Richie Valens, and The Big Bopper who were killed in a plane crash," T.N. replied with a hint of nostalgia in his voice. "And because they were so famous at the time, the day they died became known as 'the day the music died.'"

After they both ordered cheeseburgers, fries, and cream sodas, Grant said, "I've heard different stories as to why McLean named his song, 'American Pie.'"

"Yeah, so have I. There's one story that he named it after the plane, but there's no evidence that's true."

"What about naming it 'American Pie' because he was dating one of the 1959 candidates for Miss America?"

"I don't know; there are so many different stories that we may never know the truth. However, it's commonly believed that February making him shiver refers to the plane crashing in February. And they say McLean was a paperboy at the time of the crash which explains him delivering bad news on doorsteps. If true, it's difficult to believe that a possible Miss America was dating a paper boy."

"That would never happen in my world," Grant chuckled. "But didn't one person survive the crash?"

"Everyone on the plane died. However, Waylon Jennings decided against taking the flight."

"Waylon Jennings the country singer?"

"Yeah. Some say he was too sick to fly that night, others say he was afraid of flying, and some say there wasn't room for him on the plane."

"How about you; do you remember if you cried the day the music died?" Grant asked.

T.N. smiled. "I was sad, but I didn't cry. You?"

"I don't recall that day at all," Grant answered as their server brought each of them drink refills.

"Weren't you into music in '59?"

"Mostly I was into television shows."

"Oh? Like what?"

"Four great shows, *Rawhide*, *Bonanza*, *Rocky and His Friends*, and the *Untouchables* debuted in 1959, as did my favorite, *The Twilight Zone*."

T.N.'s smile turned to a look of amazement. "You can remember that?"

"1959 was a remarkable year. In addition to *Raisin in the Sun* and *The Sound of Music* opening on Broadway, the BIC ballpoint pen, pantyhose, the microchip, and the 35mm single-lens reflex camera were introduced. Fidel Castro came to power in Cuba, Giants Stadium was renamed Candlestick Park, *Lady Chatterley's Lover* was banned in the United States, and my mother bought my sister the newest doll on the marker."

"Now I'm really impressed," T.N. whistled.

"Well, I might have written a paper on 1959 for a sociology class I took in graduate school," Grant smiled, deciding to come clean on why he knew so much trivia about 1959.

T.N. laughed. "Let me guess. That doll must have been Barbie, right?"

"Barbie Roberts was her full name," Grant chuckled. A big part of their friendship had always been the game of seeing which one could "out trivia" the other.

"Do you remember Bobby Vee?"

"Sure."

"Do you know how he got his big break as a singer?"

Shaking his head, Grant confessed he didn't.

"After the plane crash, the decision was made to continue the tour. However, they needed to find another singer. They found one; a fifteen-year-old boy from Fargo, North Dakota named Bobby Vee.

Grant smiled. "Well, that explains why Vee's hit, 'Suzie Baby,' sounds so much like Buddy Holly's 'Peggy Sue' to me." Then he added, "So tell me smartass, how many cigarettes were smoked in Casablanca?"

"Twenty-two," T.N. answered with enough conviction for Grant to believe him. Shaking his head, Grant burst out laughing.

Zero To Sixty

Thou shalt not follow anyone or anything.

Celebrating his birthday in Grant's favorite Mexican restaurant, his wife asked, "What's the best thing about turning sixty?"

"Knowing that I'm now too old to spend an entire Saturday helping someone move in exchange for a slice of Little Caesar's Pizza," Grant said with a grin. "That, and the realization that there are a lot more good-looking sixty-year-old women than there used to be."

Earlier that day, Stanley, Grant's 78-year-old father, called to congratulate him on his sixtieth. Although bent under the weight of his age and molded by his life experiences, Stanley hadn't changed much in the eyes of his son. Still the family rock, he remains the standard by which Grant measures all men. An anchor in storms and an unbending oak standing against the winds of change, Stanley had become a dinosaur in his values and beliefs.

Robinsons didn't hem and haw, chit-chat, accessorize, sort M&M's by color, or refer to anything as a doozy, a humdinger, or a lollapalooza. They'd bend over backward, but never bowed. Robinsons didn't squabble; they argued. Robinsons didn't get angry; they got pissed. Robinsons were, by birth, indestructible, intractable, and impertinent. For a Robinson, the first commandment was, "Thou shalt not follow anyone or anything." If the Robinson clan had had a family crest, it would have been engraved with *non donatus rodentum anus*, Latin for, "I don't give a rat's ass!"

Stanley was two years old in 1929 when Coca-Cola was "the Pause that refreshes." Grant was twenty-three in 1969 when Coca-Cola became "the real thing." Today, during their phone conversation, Stanley summarized one of his "real things" when he said, "I trust my dog to get me up every morning at 5:30 sharp, no matter what time it is." Another of Stanley's realities is, "I can't walk for shit, can't remember shit, can't see for shit, can't hear for shit, and lately, I don't give a shit. But that's okay because I don't have anywhere I want to go, don't want to remember half the shit I know, and I've already seen and heard all the shit I can take." However, Grant, like millions of Boomers, didn't see what his family saw, didn't hear what they heard, and didn't feel what they felt. And like his fellow boomers, Grant navigated his way on his own terms or, to paraphrase Frank Sinatra, "*They did it their way.*"

Many want to be in great shape when they die. Others want to leave behind a large inheritance for their loved ones. And a large number of people want to meet death while asleep. Not Grant, and not most baby boomers he knows. Boomers want to leave behind bodies worn out from living. And when they die, they want to be wide-awake, sliding into their coffins while yelling, "Damn, that was fun!"

Blowing In The Wind

> *You've got to rattle your cage door. You've got to let them know that you're in there and that you want out. Make noise. Cause trouble. You may not win right away, but you'll sure have a lot more fun.*
>
> ~Florynce Kennedy

The Baby Boomer Generation began in 1946 as millions of young men and women returned from World War Two. Boomers were the first generation to be heavily influenced by the new technology called television, the first to live during the Cold War, and the first to grow up under the threat of nuclear war.

Although boomers are well known for being self-reliant, independent, passionate, and resourceful workaholics, they are also a generation known for their rebellious streak. With a strong belief in individualism, they aren't afraid of confrontation or shy about challenging the status quo. While being very pragmatic, they are also very idealistic, believing they could change the world. While they avoid long-term planning, they set goals for their lives and work hard to achieve them. They enjoy the challenges of life and live to make a difference. And while they tend to define their self-worth by their accomplishments, they grew up listening to rock and roll and know how to party hearty.

The answers Dylan said were "blowing in the wind," were in response to questions being asked by an entire generation of boomers. Beyond anyone's knowledge or imagination, there were people, events, and forces already at work in 1946 that would reshape American society and the Baby Boomers' view of it.

o—o

A young man named Robert F. Kennedy enlisted in the Navy while John, his older brother, was elected into the House of Representatives. Another young man, Richard Nixon, was also elected to the House of Representatives in 1946.

o—o

On August 6, 1946, Martin Luther King Jr. wrote a letter to the editor in the Atlanta Constitution stating blacks "are entitled to the basic rights and opportunities of American citizens."

o—o

Bobby Zimmerman (the future Bob Dylan) entered the first grade at the Alice School in Hibbing, Minnesota. Another boy, Lee Harvey Oswald, also entered the first grade in 1946 after his mother moved the family to Covington, Louisiana.

o—o

Bill Clinton and George W. Bush were the first two baby boomer presidents. William Jefferson Blythe III was born in Hope, Arkansas on August 19, 1946. He'd later take the last name of his stepfather, Roger Clinton. The man who would follow him as President, George Walker Bush, was born a few weeks before Bill Clinton on July 6, 1946. (The only two Presidents whose names contain the letters to spell "criminal" are William Jefferson Clinton and Richard Milhouse Nixon.)

Nat King Cole recorded "Get Your Kicks on Route 66" in 1946. Commissioned in 1926 and often called the "Mother Road," Route 66 was approximately 2,448 miles long. Connecting Chicago with Los Angeles, it crossed eight states and three time zones. Although his first encounter with Route 66 would be a piece of it on display at the Smithsonian's Museum in Washington, D.C., Grant's dream, born when he was a sixth-grader, to "motor west" on Route

66, wouldn't come true for another thirty years.

○─○

In 1946, in an effort to defeat Democratic Congressman Jerry Voorhis in California's 12th District, the Republican Party advertised in newspapers seeking a candidate "with no previous political experience." The ad specifically asked for "any young man" that was "a resident of the district, preferably a veteran" who had a "fair amount of education." It was obvious they would accept any Tom, Dick, and Harry. And that's just what they got. Answering that ad launched the political career of Dick Nixon.

○─○

In March of 1946, Rosa opened the Chat-A-Wyle Diner in Benign, New York. Grant's friends Cynthia Pratt and Ray Duncan were born that same month, followed by Graham Alexander in May and Tinker in August.

CHAPTER TWO

The Fifties

Benign Was More Than A Town; It Was A Time.

Benign was more than a town; it was a time. It was a time when Americans believed our public institutions existed to promote the general welfare and common good of society. We trusted our president to tell us the truth, we believed our government existed to serve us rather than us serving it, and it was a time before there were red or blue states instead of red, white, and blue states from coast to coast.

Benign was a time when athletes deserved to be role models when sexual promiscuity was faulted, not flaunted when good old American ingenuity could solve any problem, and when the golden rule was an accepted and practiced standard of behavior.

Benign was a time when boys knew a peewee from an aggie from a bumbo. They knew when someone was histing, what bombsies meant, and how to use a bowler. They knew that when you were talking about lagging, plunking, keepsies, mibs, cat's eye, glimmers, bloods, rubies, steely, and tiger, you were talking about playing marbles.

Benign was a time when milk was delivered fresh every morning in glass bottles by a milkman, ice was delivered by the iceman, and brushes were delivered by the Fuller Brush man. Benign was a time when we first fell in love with television, watching everything from Matt Dillon to Walter Cronkite to Jackie Gleason. It was a time when 33 1/3 rpm vinyl Gramophone records were introduced, McDonald's introduced 15-cent hamburgers, and Studebaker introduced the Lark compact.

Saturday, March 25, 2006 - The Second Chance

Grant and T.N. were having lunch at the diner. Except for the name having been changed from The Chat-A-Wyle to The Second Chance, it looked pretty much the same as it did when they'd hung out there during their high school glory days.

"The Second Chance has the best cheeseburgers in New York State," T.N. said as he slapped the bottom of a newly opened Heinz's Ketchup bottle. "Okay, mister memory, what can you tell me about Heinz Ketchup and television?"

Grant smiled. "You mean about John Heinz, the Senator from Pennsylvania who was killed in a plane crash in 1991? Then his widow, Teresa, married John Kerry, the Senator from Massachusetts, who then lost a bid for the White House to George W. Bush?"

"Actually, what I was asking about was what hit television show Heinz sponsored in the 1950s? I'll give you a hint. It was about an army outpost in North Africa."

Grant again smiled. "Great hint. You're thinking of *Captain Gallant of the Foreign Legion* staring Buster Crabbe. I watched it every Sunday night."

"Damn, you sure know your television shows," T.N. chuckled. "Let's see how well you know your Civil Rights history. Do you know the names of the three young college students murdered by the Ku Klux Klan in Mississippi in 1964 because they were helping to register black voters?"

"That would be Chaney, Schwerner, and Goodman, right?" Then, without waiting for an answer, Grant continued. "Their murders were the subject of the 1988 movie, *Mississippi Burning*."

"If you say so; I'll take your word for it. You're the retired history guy."

A Little Work Never Hurt Anyone

Work, by and large, should be given a wide berth.

~Dennis Robinson

Labor Day, the traditional end of summer, fell on Tuesday, September 2 in 1952. Back then, Grant didn't know that U.S. Marshals had killed two strikers in 1893. Nor did Grant know that President Cleveland, to appease the growing Labor Movement and its anger over those deaths, signed a bill establishing Labor Day as a national holiday to honor hard-working men and women. The only thing Grant knew about Labor Day was that school always began the next day.

Although Grant was, on a good day, an average student, as a new Benign first-grader, he loved learning and eagerly made the two-block walk to school each morning. He especially enjoyed having so many kids his age to play with each day. He also enjoyed his parents' praise when he brought home papers with a smile face or star on them. One reason for such praise might have been his inability to make it home with sad-faced papers. Had his parents discovered the secret tree-lined shortcut to school he and his friends used once they were out of sight, they would have also discovered the stash of school papers near the Niagara Mohawk Power substation in a brown sack beneath the "Danger! High Voltage" signs. As much as he liked school, there were also those times when his enthusiasm was more than he could contain, and he'd find himself standing in the corner or the hall. As was true in kindergarten, Grant didn't mind the isolation. However, he disliked having to stand next to his teacher during noon recess. Therefore, his pre-lunch behavior was always better than his post-lunch behavior.

The change in Grant's afternoon behavior didn't go unnoticed, especially by Mrs. Berry, his third-grade teacher. Mrs. Berry lived behind Pearl's Department Store in a pale-yellow house near the center of Benign. As luck would have it, Mrs. Berry and Grant's mom had become good friends. They'd met when Grant's parents agreed that Mrs. Berry could have whatever produce she wanted as payment from the garden they maintained on a lot she owned on the west side of town. Grant often wondered if his mother was talking about Mrs. Berry whenever he heard her say, "He'll lead her down the garden path." There was another phrase his parents used whenever he or Dennis, his brother, complained about working in the garden. They'd no more start moaning in protest when one of them would say, "Stop your whining; a little work never hurt anyone."

Dennis-isms

Hard work and I divorced years ago citing irreconcilable differences.

The surest way to expand your job description is to do something well.

The only people getting rich from hard work are those who have people working hard for them.

What my three ex-wives called laziness, I called pre-resting.

Who Cooks for You? Who Cooks for You?

There's no better entertainment than to entertain a new idea.

1952 was a tipping point for Grant, Benign, the United States, and the world. The first hydrogen bomb was detonated, the first Holiday Inn opened, *Mad Magazine* debuted, and Elizabeth II became the Queen of England. The Big Bang Theory and the contraceptive pill were introduced, *Anne Frank; The Diary of a Young Girl* was published in the United States, roll-on deodorant, and the transistor radio were developed. *The Guiding Light* moved from radio to television, Rocky Marciano became heavyweight champion of the world, Albert Schweitzer won the 1952 Nobel Peace Prize, Mr. Potato Head hit store shelves, Kellogg's introduced Sugar Frosted Flakes, and Robin Williams was born in Chicago. Hemingway's, *The Old Man and the Sea* and Steinbeck's *East of Eden* were published and one of the most popular movies among Baby Boomers, *High Noon* staring Gary Cooper and Grace Kelly, was released. On movie screens across the country, Will Kane stood reluctantly alone against Frank Miller, while his fellow townspeople did nothing to help.

There were four major events in 1952 that would forever change how Americans viewed war, sex, disease, and communication. The first was the detonation of a hydrogen bomb, giving birth to bomb shelters, air raid drills in schools, and the cold war. The second was the introduction of the birth control pill, opening the door to free love, the population zero movements of the sixties, and the birth of Planned Parenthood. The third was Dr. Jonas Salk's groundbreaking discovery of a vaccine for polio increasing America's faith in science. The fourth was the transistor radio, opening the door to hundreds of inventions from hearing aids to wireless communication. It also helped spread the rock 'n roll movement as boomers began listening to their own radios instead of having to compete for airtime on the family radio.

These events would eventually have their impact upon Grant, but a more immediate impact was unfolding in Washington DC. By the end of October of 1952, Senator McCarthy had gained national recognition for holding government hearings to weed out "Communist traitors" in both the government and Hollywood. Before McCarthy's witch hunts, children across the country collected money for the United Nations Children's Fund (UNICEF) on Halloween. However, because of suspicions that UNICEF might be full of communists, public schools began banning the use of the UNICEF boxes. As a result, Grant and millions of other kids enjoyed their first experience of trick or treating for candy, apples, and popcorn balls.

Two years later, in Grant's third-grade classroom, there were two black and white pictures hanging on the wall opposite the windows, one on each side of the clock. One was a painting of Washington; the other was a photograph of Lincoln. However, Mrs. Berry wouldn't allow her students to call them Washington and Lincoln. "You can call them by their full name, or you can call them President Washington and President Lincoln. However, referring to them by just their last names is disrespectful. This is true of all our Presidents. Our Presidents were elected by the people, and we all need to show our respect for them as great men and our respect for the office of the president," Mrs. Berry repeated many times. She also repeated a quote she attributed to Abraham Lincoln; *"You can fool all of the people some of the time and some of the people all the time, but you can't fool all the people all of the time."* Unfortunately, although the quote contains wisdom worth noting, Abraham Lincoln didn't say it. No one knows for sure who first said it, but many historians believe it was P. T. Barnum.

Grant liked President Lincoln's picture more than President Washington's because it was a real photograph and, although President Lincoln had a sad, overcast expression like an approaching summer storm, he looked like a friendly, gentle man. On the other hand, President Washington had a stern, judgmental look to him. It didn't matter where Grant went in the room, President Washington's eyes followed him, waiting to catch Grant misbehaving. More than a few times, as Grant was about to throw a spit wad, pass a note across the aisle, or talk during quiet time, he'd notice President Washington staring at him with such a forbidding expression that Grant didn't dare disappoint the Father of the Country.

Halloween was one of Grant's lifelong favorite celebrations. He would always fondly remember the first Halloween he went Trick or Treating. Wearing a Long Ranger Mask, he and Tonto (Crackers) ran from house to house carrying pillowcases full of the marvelous treats they'd collected. For several days afterward, Crackers insisted upon calling Grant "Ke-mo sah-bee," meaning "trusted friend." Grant also remembers how impressed he was with a visitor to his classroom that October morning. Mrs. Berry had inadvertently left a window open when she'd gone home the day before. Unless it rained, that wouldn't have been a problem because their third-grade classroom was on the second floor. That morning, Mrs. Berry stood in the doorway, whispering for them to quietly take a seat as she pointed toward the inside wall.

Grant and his classmates quietly sat in awe watching a small owl perched on none other than President Washington's picture. With its white feathers, brown eyes, and ivory-colored beak, the owl seemed right at home as it spent the morning watching one class of sightseers after another filing in and out of the room. The owl was the hit of the entire building, especially for Grant who couldn't figure out how it could turn its head almost all the way around.

Except for Christmas mornings, Friday, October 31, 1952, was the most exciting day of Grant's Wonder Years. He not only loved the owl, but he also loved the scariness of running through the crunchy leaves after dark as he went from house to house yelling, "Who cooks for you? Who cooks for you?" Grant knew he was supposed to yell "Trick or Treat," but it was more fun imitating the sound the owl had made that day. Crackers, on the other hand, insisted upon yelling, "Hi-ho, Silver! Away" as they left each yard.

Tick-Tock

I can't be good at living and good at time management at the same time.

~Clanton Delaney

All of Mrs. Berry's third graders, especially Grant, were disappointed the following Monday morning when they entered the room to find the owl was gone. They'd hoped it would take up permanent residence on top of President Washington. Seizing upon a teaching moment, Mrs. Berry had put out several books about owls and other birds of prey on the Reading Center table. The owl and those books were the birth of what would become Grant's lifelong love of birds.

By the third grade, Grant had a well-earned reputation as a clock-watcher and, between the two classroom Presidents, Mrs. Berry had a large, new wall clock. It was a General Electric with a glass cover and a red second hand. Unlike other clocks Grant had seen, the second hand on this one didn't move at a steady, even pace. Rather, the red hand would jump from one second to the next. Soon the clock became an accomplice in any number of games Grant played in his head. He wasn't only watching the minutes counting down toward lunch, gym, art, music, or dismissal time; he was getting good at closing his eyes for a specific number of seconds. He could, within a second or two, close his eyes for exactly one minute. Using his time trying to make it pass faster, he would also try to guess how long it would take Mrs. Berry to say specific terms. His two favorites were "eyes forward" and "thinking caps." Another game he enjoyed was seeing for how many seconds he could hold his breath. By the time he got to high school, Grant knew if he died in school, it would be from bubonic boredom.

I Like Ike

Ike was right, a quarter isn't worth a dime anymore.

~Brad Bodine

Wednesday, November 5, 1952 - Chat-A-Wyle Diner

"I admit we Republicans can be greedy bastards, but at least we're in touch with reality. You, Democrats, are a feeble-minded lot," Fred joked as he and Delaney took seats at their usual table. They often met for breakfast at The Chat-A-Wyle and always talked politics. That was especially true today. Both had stayed up most of the night watching the election returns. Friends since high school, they'd been arguing since the GOP nominated Eisenhower for President at their July convention. Now Eisenhower had just been elected the 34th President of the United States.

Both of them liked Ike. However, there was no way Delaney, a lifelong Democrat, could ever vote Republican. "Your boy won so the least you can do is pay for my breakfast," Delaney said with a grin as their waitress approached their booth.

Fred laughed, savoring the moment. Then, looking up he said, "Good morning, Rosa. I'll have the pancake special and my friend here will have a plate of crow and some humble pie for dessert."

"Ouch," Delaney chuckled. "I can see there will be no living with you."

"I've got to rub it in a little. You'd be riding me if Stevenson had won," Fred replied. "Regardless, Stevenson did better than Truman would have. He was wise not to run. The Korean mess and then firing MacArthur pretty much destroyed any chance he had of getting elected."

"True enough. And given Eisenhower's war record, I doubt anyone could have defeated him. With 44% of the vote, Stevenson did as well as could be expected. I just hope nothing happens to Ike. The last thing we need is Nixon as President."

"What's wrong with Nixon?" Fred asked. "He ran a good campaign, especially when he talked about his wife's Republican cloth coat."

"I can't believe you fell for that hook, line, and sinker," Delaney said as his smile faded. Although Delaney was able to see the humor in politics, he was first, foremost, and forever a Yellow Dog Democrat. Except during a lapse of sanity and voting for Dewey in '48, Delaney's father and his father's father made no bones about voting for a yellow dog before they'd vote for a Republican. Delaney's ancestors had been among the first to settle in the Virginia colony and hadn't voted Republican since Lincoln and the Civil War.

"Talk about cheesy. And then that whole thing with his dog; I've never seen the likes of it," Delaney continued.

"You mean Checkers? I thought that was the high point of that speech. It showed he was a regular guy, not some intellectual millionaire like Stevenson."

"Come on, you can't be serious. That whole thing about his daughter naming the dog Checkers because of its black with white spots; as I said, the whole thing was cheesy."

"He might have overdone it a little, but all in all, it put questions about his honesty to bed. And it kept him on the ticket," Fred countered.

"You don't think he's honest, do you? Look at how he got elected to the Senate. He beat his woman opponent by falsely suggesting she was connected to the Communist

Party. He called her the 'Pink Lady,' insinuating she was a pinko commie. Hell, he even said she was 'pink right down to her underwear.' No wonder she began calling him 'Tricky Dick.'"

"Say what you want, Nixon did a good job on the House Un-American Activities Committee. He's the one who broke open the Alger Hiss thing. He might be cheesy, but he's true red, white, and blue. Hell, his great-grandfather fought and died at Gettysburg."

"Be careful, these plates are hot," Rosa said as she approached their table just in time to hear Delaney say, "You mark my words, Nixon can't be trusted any farther than my dog can shit a walnut."

Noble-isms

Democrats want to tell you what to do while Republicans want to tell you what to think.

Under the Democrats, everyone lies to everyone. Under the Republicans, it's just the opposite.

Democracy gives politicians the right to do shit that's not right to do.

All The Time. Everywhere. Be Cautious. Take Care.

Life is fraught with delays, disappointments, disasters, and lined with an overabundance of annoying bastards.

~Dexter Hammond

August 6, 1953

In 1953, Jacqueline Bouvier married John F. Kennedy, Cinemascope was introduced by 20th Century Fox, L. Ron Hubbard founded The Church of Scientology, Sir Edmund Hillary and Tenzing Norgay were the first to reach the summit of Mount Everest, and *Casino Royale*, the first James Bond novel, was published. Among the most popular songs of 1953 were, "Crying in the Chapel" by Elvis Presley, "The Doggie in the Window" by Patti Page, "That's Amore" by Dean Martin, and "Don't Let the Stars Get in Your Eyes" by Perry Como. Invented in 1913 by John Lloyd Wright, Frank Lloyd Wright's son, Lincoln Logs were a favorite children's toy in 1953.

After six decades, many of Grant's memories have grown slippery, but not those of the summer day that taught him it's through love that we most deeply feel another's pain. Seared in his memory, he can still recall how that day began, how it ended, and the sights, sounds, and smells in between. He remembers the sweet ozone freshness following the morning rain, the smiling red rooster, the hot beach sand, the waxpaper encased tuna sandwiches, the fresh baked cookies, the empty coffee can, the sawdust-covered ice, the honeybees, the goulash, the sluggish evening air, and the pain of skin peeling off like the top layer of an onion. But mostly he remembers his mother's liquid dark eyes, the source of each drop of undeserved guilt running down her cheeks.

Forty-four days short of his seventh birthday, Grant entered Thursday, August 6, 1953, angry with Danny Burgess, the Channel 7 weatherman, because he thought the weatherman determined the weather. Though steady, it was no longer a heavy rain as Grant watched the hands on the red rooster kitchen clock slip past 10 a.m. Grant was depending upon his grandfather's adage, "Rain before seven, stop before eleven," to clear the heavens within the hour.

Somewhere around 10:45, Grant's faith in his grandfather solidified as the sun peeked and then burst out of hiding. It came quickly to stay and was bright enough for Grant's mother to honor her promise of a picnic at Crystal Lake. The red rooster's noon smile matched Grant's own as he, his mother, and brother loaded lunch, towels, and blue-patched black inner tubes into the car. A twelve-mile drive later, as their mother covered a rickety wooden picnic table with a red and white checked plastic tablecloth, Dennis and Grant raced across the sand toward the beckoning blueness. For over an hour the beach and anchored diving raft belonged to twenty or so local kids until two busloads of kids arrived for their summer school-sponsored swimming lessons. Surrendering to the interlopers, those not there for the lessons were forced into exile by a whistle-blowing warden.

After trying to cross the beach with as little sand as possible sticking to their wet feet, Dennis and Grant ate their lunch while wrapped in their Superman and Batman beach towels. There were smiles and giggles all around as they enjoyed potato chips, pickles, tuna sandwiches, carrot sticks, their mom's fresh-squeezed lemonade, and fresh chocolate chip cookies for dessert. To Grant, there were only two kinds of cookies; one was chocolate chip, and the other wasn't.

In the 1950s, lunch at the beach was always followed by a mandatory one-hour wait before reentering the water. No one seemed to know exactly why, but somehow waiting sixty minutes prevented cramps that could cause kids to drown. Always prepared, Maretta pulled an empty Maxwell House coffee can from her bag of tricks and initiated a game of kick the can. Almost immediately, several of the other kids joined the game as they waited for the intruders to return to their yellow rides home. Once back in the water, the remaining afternoon passed quickly. All too soon, Maretta waved them ashore. After one, perhaps two, last jumps off the raft, Dennis and Grant again tried crossing the beach with as little sand as possible sticking to their feet. Life was good.

Somewhere between getting home and supper, Dennis and Grant joined the neighbor kids surrounding the slow-moving ice truck coming down their street. With a thick leather pad protecting his shoulder, they followed the iceman in and out of kitchen after kitchen as they watched him deposit a large block of ice in the top of each icebox. At the end of the street, the iceman finally responded to their pleas and, cleaning the sawdust off one of the ice blocks, he treated each of them to a small slice of winter to savor on a hot summer day.

That evening's dinner entree was changed to goulash after Grant's father called to say he had to work a double shift at the paper mill. Maretta nearly always made goulash on double shift nights because it was both Stanley's favorite and easy to reheat after midnight. Except when the family went to the Black River Drive-in and once when he stayed up on New Year's Eve to watch Guy Lombardo and his Royal Canadians, Grant wasn't allowed up past 8:30 PM. But that night the red rooster and Grant would welcome the new day together.

After eating out the hamburger, Grant pushed the mushy elbow macaroni around on the plate until it looked small enough for his mother to say he'd eaten enough. Once free from the table, Dennis and Grant raced the sinking sun trying to catch the last of the honeybees before it got dark. Using Miracle Whip jars with air holes punched in the blue and white lids, the trick was to pop off the lid, scoop up a bee from a flower without being stung, and close the lid before the previous captives could escape. Their bee hunting expedition ended when three flashes of the back porch light signaled it was time to come in for the night. At Maretta's insistence, they left their jars outside with the lids off so the bees could escape safely. Next came the nightly ritual of cast iron tub baths, pajamas, combed hair so it wouldn't dry messy, and one radio program before bedtime.

To Grant's future grandkids, BC would stand for before cable. To his kids, it would stand for before color. However, on that summer evening, Grant's family was still years from owning their first television. On those nights when his parents felt their behavior justified it, Dennis and Grant were allowed to "watch" one program on the radio before going to bed. The red rooster said it was eight o'clock as they tuned in just in time to hear, "Out of the blue of the western sky comes Sky King." Although Grant liked *Gangbusters, Gunsmoke, Death Valley Days, Sergeant Preston of the Yukon* ("I arrest you in the name of the Crown."), and The *Shadow*, his favorite program was *Sky King*. Each episode began with, "All the time. Everywhere. Be cautious. Take care." It would only be a matter of minutes before those words would return to haunt both Grant and his mother.

Shortly after World War II, to house the growing crop of baby boomers, America invented suburbia. Although the two-story house Grant's family lived in was already old in 1953, the kitchen's location was the same as in the new suburban subdivision homes. The women who'd filled the factories during the war had been replaced by the returning troops so, except for teachers, nurses, and telephone operators, about the only women working outside the home in Benign, were single, divorced, or widowed. Designing the new homes with the kitchen in the back allowed moms across America to work in the kitchen while they watched over their children playing in the backyard. It was also a subliminal message to women that they need not look to the front door as a portal leading to a sense of value, self-worth, or purpose. Except for her one flaw of working outside the home, Grant's mom was the picture of the perfect fifties' wife and mother. While Dennis and Grant were in school, Maretta worked Monday mornings cleaning the Methodist Church and Thursday and Friday mornings cleaning the homes of two elderly couples. However, she escaped the criticisms afforded women who tried to combine a job with motherhood because her work involved the church, the elderly, and housecleaning.

As any mother can tell you, multitasking is not a new concept. With eggs boiling on the stove, Maretta mopped and waxed the kitchen floor as she half-listened to the radio with Grant and Dennis. With the floor done, instead of listening to a young Mike Wallace, who was just beginning his career as a TV journalist, doing the Peter Pan Peanut Butter commercial, she placed a basket of clean clothes fresh from the clothesline on the kitchen table. Then, using a longneck Pepsi bottle with a cork sprinkler in it, she began turning desert-dry clothes into small damp logs, rolled and stacked for ironing. Following the program, Grant was flying high as he rounded the corner from the living room, banked through the kitchen doorway, and, with outstretched arms as wings, buzzed the kitchen. With his engine sputtering, Grant was attempting an emergency landing in front of the open pantry door when he crashed on the eve of what would become several hours of pain and regret.

With her back to Grant, Maretta turned into his flight path. Unable to stop on the newly waxed floor, Grant hit her hard enough to knock her off her feet, making it impossible for her to maintain control of the pan of boiling water and hardboiled eggs. Although she wasn't hurt or burned, she wasn't able to reach Grant in time to prevent him from frantically pulling off his pajama top, taking red-hot skin from his face, neck, shoulder, and chest with it. More than the pain, Grant vividly remembers the terrified look in his mother's eyes. He can't now remember which of them said "I'm sorry" more, him for running in the house and knocking his mother down or Maretta as she blamed herself for his burns.

With the nearest doctor a frantic thirty-minute drive away, Maretta called Mrs. Lonsdale instead, a neighbor wise in remedies and homemade poultices. With the red rooster cackling every half hour, Maretta would hold Grant tight in her arms as Mrs. Lonsdale applied wet towels laced with a terrible smelling collection of ingredients she said would prevent scaring. Each application generated more screams, and it was well past midnight when Stanley found Maretta holding Grant, both still crying. Grant didn't know which of them was in greater pain, but Maretta was the one who carried the scars. It wasn't until Grant became a father that he understood how much his mother had wished she'd been burned instead.

Say, Kids, What Time Is It?

Let's give a rousing cheer,
Cause Howdy Doody's here,
It's time to start the show,
So kids let's go!

Grant's favorite bread, along with most everyone else his age, was Wonder Bread, but not because it built strong bodies eight ways. Rather, Wonder Bread's popularity with children had more to do with the future Captain James T. Kirk of the Starship Enterprise and his Doodyville friends. In 1954, long before he began his five-year mission to discover strange, new worlds, William Shatner was known to millions of baby boomers as Ranger Bill on the *Howdy Doody* television show. One of Ranger Bill's tasks was to explain to millions of children, and their parents, about the nutritional value of Wonder Bread. By the time Grant graduated from high school, he'd eaten so many tuna sandwiches on Wonder Bread that he was sure some of those tuna must have known each other.

Originally called *Puppet Playhouse*, *Howdy Doody* was the first television network series to be broadcast in color, the first to reach 2,000 episodes, and, thanks to Buffalo Bob, it was one of the first to understand the potential of television to market products like Colgate, Welch's Grape Jelly, and Wonder Bread directly to children.

At nineteen cents a loaf and encased in its famous red, yellow, and blue balloon-covered wrapper, Wonder Bread had been building strong bodies since 1921. Elmer Kline, while visiting an International Balloon Festival at the Indianapolis Motor Speedway, was inspired by the brightly colored hot air balloons filling the sky. He said he named the new bread his company was introducing Wonder Bread after the "awe and wonderment" he felt at the festival.

"How do you do?" was a popular American greeting and the source for the name of the freckled-faced cowboy puppet America knew as Howdy Doody. He had forty-eight freckles, one for each of the forty-eight states. Although baby boomer memories are now beginning to spring leaks, they'll never forget Flub-a-Dub, Cawabonga, Chief Thunderthud, Princess Summerfall Winterspring, and Buffalo Bob. One of the most popular residents of Doodyville was Clarabell the Clown with his honking horns and squirting seltzer. In the show's history, the only time Clarabell ever spoke was when he said, "Goodbye kids," in the final episode. Bob Keeshan, the first Clarabell, would later entertain millions of baby boomers as Captain Kangaroo.

Regardless of where he sat in school, Grant did his best at being overlooked. A poor reader, Grant's worst fear was being called upon to read in front of the class. Nothing destroyed his self-confidence and feelings of self-worth more than stumbling his way through a paragraph with the teacher having to supply the words he didn't know. His second fear was being called upon to solve a math problem on the blackboard with his classmates watching and waiting. He was sure, in addition to thinking he was dumb, that they were making fun of his clothes, his skinny legs, and oversized ears.

It wasn't until the sixth grade, after three years of advanced readiness seminars (remedial reading) when Mr. Borcey turned Grant on to American History, that Grant did the unthinkable; he read his first non-comic book for fun. That first book, *Robert E. Lee and the Road to Honor* was immediately followed by *Davy Crockett, Custer's Last Stand, Wyatt Earp: U.S. Marshall*, and *The Swamp Fox of the Revolution*. Grant's love of books and American History would be a lifelong affair.

Welcome to Indian River

School boards are to education as dogs are to trees.

~Stanley Robinson

The first issue of *Playboy*, featuring nude pictures of Marilyn Monroe, was published in 1953. Two years later, while playing in his Uncle Ray's garage, Grant found a copy of *Playboy* that generated far more questions than it answered. Although he was only eight and a half years old, he can still remember his first *Playboy* bunny. Miss January of 1955, Bettie Page, was posing in front of a Christmas tree wearing nothing but a smile and a red Santa hat. Grant can remember thinking that he wanted to do something to her but had no idea what.

Later that year, on September 20 (one day after Grant turned nine), ABC aired the first episode of *Cheyenne*. Produced by William Orr, *Cheyenne's* 108 episodes ran from 1955 to 1962 and were the first hour-long Western on television. The series, filmed at Warner Brothers, made Clint Walker a huge star and a television Western icon. The success of *Cheyenne* soon led the way for shows like *Sugarfoot, Bronco, Lawman, 77 Sunset Strip,* and another of Grant's favorites, *Maverick*.

Because his mother loved Clint Walker so much, Grant was especially pleased when he met Clint and his wife Susan in Kanab, Utah in 2005. What an honor it was to talk with them again in 2008, and yet again in 2011. Since their conversation in 2008, Grant and Susan have exchanged emails regarding both Clint and the *Cheyenne* DVDs now available from Clint's website. One of Grant's prized possessions is an autographed picture he took of Clint and Susan; Clint also posted the picture on his website. Now in his eighties, Clint is still ruggedly handsome with a quick wit and a great sense of humor.

1955 was a life-changing year for Grant for yet another reason. The citizens of Benign, Evans Mills, Antwerp, and Philadelphia voted on Thursday, June 30, 1955, to consolidate the four village school systems to create the Indian River Central School District with a new Junior High/High School to be built in Philadelphia. The four pre-existing village schools would then be converted to elementary schools. The new building opened on September 2, 1958.

About all Grant can recall about that June 30th date is the anger his father expressed to Clancy Sheridan about the additional taxes it would take to build a new 7-12 High School. Clancy lived three houses down the street from Grant's family, was the newest member of the School Board, and had been the one to cast the deciding vote for centralization of the four school districts.

We Are Taught to Hate Those We Hate by Those We Love

Words are at most powerful tool and weapon. In themselves, they're only sounds and have no meaning other than as symbols for what they represent. Their power comes from the meanings we attach to them. Therefore, obscenity isn't found in vocabulary, but within the heart.

~Dennis Robinson

It was in 1955 that Rosa Parks refused to give up her seat on a bus to a white man, Disneyland opened, Ford introduced the Thunderbird, James Dean was killed in an automobile accident, Ray Kroc started McDonald's, and Tappan manufactured the first home microwave oven. It was also the year that Quaker Oats introduced Instant Oatmeal, Johnson and Johnson introduced the first baby shampoo, Congress voted that all U.S. currency would be inscribed with "In God We Trust, *The Village Voice* began publication, and President Eisenhower held the first televised press conference.

Grant's mother had a way of explaining things to him, so he'd understand. When she made a point, it usually pricked for weeks. Grant's family lived a block from the Benign Elementary School, where he'd just finished the fourth grade. Danny, one of only two black kids living in Benign, was a year younger and lived in the same neighborhood. However, they weren't neighbors. Black kids in Benign in the summer of 1955 didn't have neighbors. Nor were they called black. Back then they were called colored or niggers and most everyone said they were too lazy to work, too stupid to learn, and too different to be trusted.

Nearly every day during the summer, Grant, T.N., Moose, Tinker, and their friends could be found playing baseball on one of the school ball diamonds. All of them had been told not to play with Danny and, except for baseball, they didn't. Baseball didn't count. Danny was one of the best players and his owning a bat, ball, and two gloves also had a great deal to do with their selective color blindness. Another boy, Don, a Hawaiian boy, also lived in Grant's neighborhood. None of the guys thought of Don as being black, just a little over melaninated. Although he was darker than Danny, Grant and the other guys were allowed to play with him. They didn't. Back then, kids were taught not to trust Hawaiians either. However, Grant and the guys would have played with Don if he had owned a bat and ball. To them, when it came to baseball, skin color was less important than ability, and ability was defined as what you brought to the game.

Grant's first mistake was in forgetting that his mother didn't share his appreciation for Danny's baseball abilities and letting it slip that he was playing with the guys. Somehow, Danny's playing with them seemed different than them playing with him. It wasn't. Grant's mother started shouting (always a bad sign) things about what the neighbors would think, diseases he'd catch from niggers, and what his father would do when he got home. Trying to talk his way out of it was Grant's second mistake. The faster he talked the slower his mother listened until he was talking so fast, she couldn't hear anything he said. Grant soon realized she didn't care that one of Danny's gloves was a real catcher's mitt, the only one Grant had ever seen. She didn't care that Danny could always bat you in. She didn't care that Danny was the best pitcher. Then came her simple question, the worst kind of question. Grant responded with the plain truth, the best kind of answer. When she asked Grant if he thought his nigger friend was as good as he was, Grant answered yes, thinking she was referring to how well Danny played baseball. She wasn't. Grant didn't know which hurt more, the look on his mother's face or the slap he received across his. Grant's mother had a way of explaining things to him so he understood.

Benign's Labor Pains

> *I don't feel we did wrong in taking this great country away from them. There were great numbers of people who needed new land, and the Indians were selfish to keep it for themselves.*
>
> ~John Wayne

On January 4, 1800, James Bodine convinced the Antwerp Land Company to sell him 220,000 acres of land that would one day include the town of Benign. A Frenchman by birth, James had come to America with Marquis de Lafayette to fight in the Revolutionary War. After the war, instead of returning to France, he married Remembrance Miller, a Puritan woman from Boston, Massachusetts. Remembrance, Relief, Repentance, Faithful, Charity, and Patience were common Puritan names at the time.

During the early days, the new settlement was called High Falls. Later, when James Bodine began dividing the settlement into individual lots, he changed the name to Benign, naming it after his infant daughter. Other French families moving into the area around Benign also gave their names to their settlements, including LaFargeville, Depauville, and Deferiet.

The glaciers from the last ice age weren't kind to the future farmers of Northern New York, especially to those in Jefferson County, and, in particular, to Benign. They carried away most of the topsoil, deposited large numbers of rocks and boulders, and gouged out large depressions as they moved south. When they later retreated north, they dropped their rocks and boulders while the melting glacier snow filled the deep gorges with fresh water to give Benign an abundance of beautiful lakes.

Benign's unique location accounts for its immense attraction for those looking for a place to live. In addition to the Indian River running through it, Benign is nicknamed the "Land of Lakes" because there are twelve lakes within its township boundaries. At 300 feet above sea level, Benignians enjoy four distinct seasons with a yearly average rainfall of 40 inches and a yearly average snowfall of 114 inches. On the Robinson Oxbow Road farm, about a hundred yards behind the barn was a metal stake embedded in the rock marking the highest point in Jefferson County.

The majority of Benign's long-time citizens were skeptical of progress, religious by nature, and Republican by (blue) blood. An equal mixture of Roman Catholics and Protestants, most of these Benignians have a family Bible where they keep a written record of births, deaths, marriages, and secret family recipes.

The Nick of Time

It was the last and best money-making enterprise I was involved in during sixth grade, my best and last year of elementary school.

It was originally a four-man operation. Tinker was our bookie, Moose was our vet, Crackers was our banker, and I was the supplier, supplying both the "horses" and "birds." However, it later became a three-man operation when Tinker was suspended from school for several days for selling small pieces of his mother's broken bedroom mirror. Instead of using it to send "Indian" signals, one of his fourth-grade customers was caught using it trying to look up Miss Dabb's dress.

Tinker was a good choice for our bookie. Best known for kicking a rock to school every day, everyone liked and trusted him. Tinker was a quiet boy, seldom saying more than a few words at a time. The rumor, which we wanted to believe, was that he was part Indian on his mother's side. Tinker would construct a new racetrack every day. Using a plastic souvenir plate with a picture of Niagara Falls on it, Tinker would trace a large circle on a sheet of paper. Then, after dividing the circle into several nearly equal sections (racing lanes), we were ready to open the betting windows.

Moose, the biggest kid in the sixth grade because he was old enough to be in the eighth grade, was in charge of running the races. Moose kept our horses and birds inside small plastic earplug boxes Tinker got from Tina, his older sister. She worked as a lifeguard but later became famous for doing headlight dancing for soldiers from Fort Drum. Except for the old Ford on blocks in their backyard, Tinker's family didn't own a car. One night Tinker's dad asked my father for a ride to work. Tinker's dad worked nights as a mechanic for a trucking company in Alexandria Bay, about twelve miles from where we lived. My father said I could ride along because it wasn't a school night and because I liked looking at the lights on the Thousand Island Bridge to Canada. However, while parked in front of Tinker's house waiting for his dad to come out, Tinker's sister suddenly appeared in our headlights and began taking off her clothes. By the time my father managed to get us out of there, I'd seen enough of Tinker's sister to make me the center of attention for several days at school.

We held races before and after school and during recess. To race, students could buy a horse from Moose or capture and break in their own. A horse was a horsefly and breaking it in meant clipping its wings. We usually raced three or four horses at a time. After placing his or her nickel bets with Tinker, each jockey placed his horse in the center of the circle. Unable to fly, the horses would walk around on the paper. The first horse to make it to the outside of the circle without going outside its lane was the winner. If a horse left its lane, its jockey could return it as long as he didn't advance it down the lane.

I don't know how much we won; we won most of the time. It was less work and more profitable than the lemonade stand my brother and I ran for the two days it took the neighborhood kids to drink us out of business. It was less work and more profitable than picking and selling blackberries to Clock's Grocery Store. It was less work and more profitable than my attempts at selling sweet corn, strawberries, and baby rabbits. It was also less work and more profitable than weeding Mrs. Huddleston's flower garden or baby-sitting old lady Lonsdale's cats. It was even more profitable than the retail candy business.

Benign, with a population of about nine hundred, could only support two small grocery stores. The largest, located in the center of town, was Clock's Grocery. The other was Pratt's gas station located on the edge of town. Between them, they controlled most of Benign's retail candy business until I began operating my store out of my desk at school.

Every Friday night, after supper, our family made the twenty-five-mile drive to Watertown, a city of about thirty-five thousand, to shop at the A & P. I would buy large bags of candy and resell them by the piece at or below Benign prices and still make a handsome profit. I was doing well until Mr. Fields, our principal, put me out of business by allowing the Student Council to begin financing its projects with a lunch hour candy sale.

My experience and reputation for getting candy plus living on a farm with an unlimited supply of horseflies helped make me the perfect choice as the supplier of horses and birds. However, within a few weeks, our classmates lost interest in horsefly racing. That's when Tinker came up with horsefly flying. Instead of Moose clipping their wings, we tied short pieces of thread to each fly, allowing their owners to fly them around on a leash. With the thread often invisible, the sight of kids flying their flies was very amusing. Because the flies only lived a couple of hours, we'd often sell several birds a day. I sold as many birds as possible before lunch, so I'd have enough money to buy candy from the Student Council during the lunch recess.

In many ways, I think being a kid forty years ago was more fun than being a kid today. Although we had more responsibilities and expectations than today's youth, we had less pressure and stress. We also had nicknames. Except for shortened forms of their names, like Jim and

Chris, today's kids seldom have nicknames. We got our nicknames from our peers, and they stayed with us for years. I was given the nickname "General" in the sixth grade and, years later, that nickname was printed in my senior yearbook next to my picture. Now, looking back through forty years, names like Moose, Tinker, and Crackers add texture to my memories and memories to my list of blessings.

Alis Volat Propriis

Force, violence, pressure, or compulsion with a view to conformity, are both uncivilized and undemocratic.

~Mohandas Gandhi

Grant's first experience with convictions occurred in the sixth grade when Cynthia Pratt came unanticipated and unwanted into his life, as most life-changing people tend to do. It was love at first sight as newfound hormones whispered her name. It took me days to muster the courage to write her. She wasn't impressed and, giving me a look with no future in it, she read and then wadded my hopes into a small ball. That pattern of writing, reading, and wadding was repeated many times as I taught her about persistence, and she taught me about rejection. Over the next decade, she would teach him much, including opening a world of mysteries with love's first kiss.

However, Cindy's first and perhaps most lasting lesson came shortly after she moved to Benign from Alexander Bay. She had made and worn a badge that said something like, "Bay Beat," while everyone else wore one saying, "Beat the Bay." Grant can't now remember what sport their schools were playing, but he remembers well the harassment she received over her badge and that, by the age of ten, she had the strength of character to stand up for what she believed. A few years later, in high school Latin, Grant began describing her as, *alis volat propriis*, meaning, "She flies on her own wings." Grant was so impressed with her that, over fifty years later, he can still remember the poodle skirt she was wearing that day. Cynthia was his first example of what Robert Ingersoll meant when he wrote, "It is a blessed thing that in every age someone has had the individuality enough and courage enough to stand by his own convictions."

It wasn't until his tenth-grade history teacher required his students to sign an oath swearing they wouldn't cheat on his exams that Grant was first convicted by a conviction. Grant had not cheated, nor did he intend to the afternoon he refused to sign the oath. He was sent to the principal's office and required to remain there until he changed his mind. He returned to class three days later after the principal finally agreed that anyone willing to cheat would also be willing to lie.

Stanley-ism

Standing by others requires you first to be willing to stand by yourself.

The conductor faces the music, not the audience.

The man who gives in when he knows he's right is either a coward or married.

Monday, September 1, 1958

> *Wisdom knows the difference between the buzzard and the eagle. Sometimes you need to wait patiently and sometimes you have to go out and kill something.*
>
> ~Tnarg Nosinbor

Benign's population of seven hundred adults remained constant from 1900 to the mid-fifties. As the Baby Boomers were about to enter school, many families fled the Watertown city schools for the quaint, quiet "Mayberry" life in one of the surrounding villages, especially Benign. This influx resulted in a larger tax base, but it also generated a need for more classrooms and more teachers. At first, the villages put off the inevitable by building additions to their existing buildings. Finally, as the villages realized they couldn't keep up with the growing number of new-abouts, they began consolidating to form larger school districts.

On Monday, September 1, 1958, one day before Grant entered the seventh grade in the new Junior High/High School in Philadelphia, his neighborhood gathered at the Lonsdales for a Labor Day potluck picnic. Although his parents had moved to the farm earlier that summer, they'd been invited to return for the celebration. Grant's going to a new school and his upcoming twelfth birthday were favorite topics of conversation that sunny afternoon, but the big attention getter at the picnic was the two Hula-Hoops the Slater kids brought. The big must-have toy of 1958, everyone, both young and old, had to try out the latest fad sweeping the country. Made of durable plastic, Richard Knerr and Arthur "Spud" Melin sold twenty million of them in the first six months. They also marketed the Wham-O slingshot and would later introduce the Frisbee.

Also in 1958, the Grammy Awards, the BankAmericard (which would later become the Visa card), Coco Puffs, the Chevy Impala, Sweet n' Low, Friskies (the first dry cat food), and Japan's new Datsun made their debut. "Rice-a-Roni The San Francisco Treat," Crest's "Look Ma! No cavities!" and the Jolly Green Giant's "Ho, Ho, Ho, Good things from the garden," became the most popular television commercials. *Dr. Zhivago* was published, NASA was created, skateboards and the first pacemaker were invented, and The John Birch Society was formed,

The first Pizza Hut opened in 1958 in Wichita, Kansas, National Airlines offered the first domestic jet-airline service, Pope Pius XII died, Roy Campanella was paralyzed in an automobile accident, and the price of first-class postage stamps went from three to four cents. Drive-in movies reached their peak in popularity in 1958 with 4,063 screens, Perry Como was awarded the first-ever Gold Record for "Catch A Falling Star," Americans ate four hundred million frozen potpies, and over forty-five million American homes had a television.

Grant's greatest disappointment on that first day in his new school was not being in any of Cindy's classes. Still submerged in the joys and pain of first love, he looked for her all day. He did manage to get a glimpse of her at lunch but was far too shy to approach her. That afternoon, instead of getting on his new bus, bus 9, he followed Cindy from a safe distance and boarded her bus, bus 12. When they reached Benign, Cindy and the other townies were dropped off at the main intersection before the remaining kids were delivered to the surrounding farms. After riding two seats behind her, he got off at her stop, still too shy to speak to her. Like a constant itch, he couldn't scratch, Cindy didn't give him a passing glance, but being that close to her was worth the two-mile walk home.

The Fakes, The Flakes, and The Famous

Normal is not something to aspire to; it's something to get away from.

~Jodi Foster

Once or twice a year, Uncle Ray returned to Benign from his new life in California. Actually, he'd become an ex-uncle three years earlier when Grant's aunt divorced him for alienation of affection. At thirteen, Grant didn't understand exactly what alienation of affection meant but sensed it had something to do with Uncle Ray also having a girlfriend. Other than Grant, the family disliked Uncle Ray. As is the case with many divorces, family and friends had to pick a side and Uncle Ray lost thumbs down. One afternoon Grant had heard his father say, "Having Ray here to help with the haying is like having two hired hands gone."

Although it was a hit following its release in 1953, it would be another six years before Grant would see Marlon Brando in *The Wild One*. Now in the seventh grade, Grant didn't yet understand why millions of baby boomers' favorite lines from the movie came when Johnny (Brando) was asked, "What are you rebelling against?" and Johnny replies, "Whaddya got?"

Grant, like a few million other boys in 1959, lusted for a black leather motorcycle jacket. Less than a month after expressing his desire to own one to his Uncle Ray, his uncle showed up at the farm with one in hand. Uncle Ray usually returned from California bearing small gifts for Grant and Dennis, but a black leather jacket for Grant (It had eight zippered pockets, including one near each wrist.) was over the top. Although his uncle worked as a security guard at a bus depot, Grant thought Ray was the embodiment of "hip" because he wore clothes the "hicks" of Upstate New York wouldn't see in the stores for months.

Uncle Ray was also a source of the latest cool lingo. Uncle Ray introduced Grant to bodacious, copasetic, top banana, solid, far out, a real blast, shades, looking for a rumble, right on, hang loose, fuzz, dig it, let's book, going ape, and I've got dibs. However, Uncle Ray was soon outmatched by Kookie, a hip, hair-combing "beatnik" on *77 Sunset Strip*, television's first hour-long private eye show. Thanks to Kookie, every kid in the country was up on the latest cool lingo. Make no bones about it; Grant's parents weren't impressed with the next generation's slang. Although they had their own lingo like spiffy, monkey shines, bee's knees, cat's pajamas, carry a torch, pushover, and gams, his parents and their friends wondered what was to become of their kids.

Grant's parents, especially his father, weren't impressed with the black leather jacket and considered California to be the home of fakes, flakes, and people famous for their immoral behavior. As far as the parents of Benign were concerned, motorcycle jackets and cool lingo were a slippery slope to hell. And as far as Uncle Ray was concerned, morality was its own punishment.

CHAPTER THREE

Welcome to the Neighborhood

Benign Was More Than a Town; It Was a Time.

Benign was more than a town; it was a moment in time before movies needed to be rated, before tamper-proof containers, before using drugs got you arrested, before security checks at airports, gated communities, motion and metal detectors, and before our lives were invaded by ringing smart phones.

Benign was a time when a simple handshake was the only guarantee anyone needed, when families ate together around the kitchen table instead of around the television, and when stores were closed on Sunday. It was a time when doctors made house calls, men tipped their hats when meeting a woman and took them off when entering a building, and it was a time when, if you did something wrong, you stood up and took your medicine.

Benign was more than a town, it was roller skate keys, soda jerks, 45 rpm records, cartoons before the main attraction, washtub ringers, pedal pushers, and Buster Brown Shoes. It was donkey basketball, *Beany and Cecil*, Sunday afternoon drives, cooties, 10-cent allowances, 5-cent candy bars and 5-cents a scoop ice cream cones, drive-in movies, Carling Black Label Beer, yellow Quaker State Oil signs, gym uniforms, fallout shelters, spitballs, men giving up their seats on a bus to a woman, Nash automobiles, and "I'll be a monkey's uncle."

Benign was a time when a girl was considered an old maid if she wasn't married by age twenty-five when you broke your mother's back if you stepped on a crack, and making wisecracks would result in your mother telling you not to be a smart-aleck because you were being snippy, forward, flip, sassy, or fresh. Benign was also a time when small towns had weekly newspapers devoted to local news, want ads, and personals.

Saturday, March 25, 2006 - The Second Chance

"Did you ever believe in rock 'n' roll?" Grant asked T.N. as they continued discussing McLean's "American Pie".

"A few times," T.N. replied with a wide grin. "How about you?"

"Oh, once or twice," Grant chuckled. "In fact, you and I believed in rock 'n' roll with some of the same girls, and, as I recall, you had a habit of getting the last dance."

"Good looks and charm always win out over substance," T.N. laughed. "How about the book of love; did you help write it?"

Smiling, Grant replied, "No, but I plagiarized a few lines."

"Really? All I managed was a couple of footnotes," T.N. joked. Then he continued with, "In verse two, McLean asks about who wrote the book of love and if we have faith in God above. Perhaps his question refers to the Monotones hit about the book of love. And I think his question about God above is a reference to the Sunday School song about Jesus loving us because the Bible tells us so."

"Sounds logical," Grant responded. "Then does his question about believing in rock 'n' roll refer to the song, 'Do You Believe in Magic?' by The Lovin' Spoonful?"

"Many think so. And perhaps McLean was asking if Holly's, Valens's, and The Big Bopper's music could save our mortal souls."

Summertime and the Living Was Easy

Of all the topics of discussion on the Lonsdale's front porch during the 1958 Labor Day picnic, the growing Civil Rights Movement wasn't one of them. Had it been discussed; it wouldn't have found any sympathetic ears in Grant's neighborhood. Except for the annual Jefferson County Fair with its several black employees, most Benignians had little or no contact with "colored" people. They certainly had little or no sympathy for their struggle for the same rights and freedoms white America enjoyed. Therefore, it wasn't surprising that few, if any, Benignians had more than a passing interest in what they would view as just another stabbing in a Harlem department store.

Just nineteen days after the Lonsdale picnic and one day after Grant's twelfth birthday, Martin Luther King Jr. was signing copies of his first book, *Stride Toward Freedom: The Montgomery Story*, when he was nearly stabbed to death with a letter opener. He was sitting at the autograph table when Izola Ware Curry, a black woman, asked him if he was Martin Luther King. When he replied he was, she buried the letter opener deep in his chest where it rested against his aorta. After an extremely delicate operation, the doctors told King that the slightest movement would have punctured his aorta and he would have drowned in his blood.

Like most of the homes in Benign, the houses in Grant's neighborhood had large porches. Several of them were "wraparound" porches running across the front and down one side of the house. These porches became the neighborhood gathering spots from early spring until late fall. After supper (the evening meal was rarely called dinner), families took turns going for evening walks, traveling from porch to porch around the block. It was an informal arrangement, with families taking turns hosting. Hosts provided hot coffee, ice tea, lemonade, and an assortment of fresh-baked cookies for their guests. Store-bought cookies were okay for family use but were considered an insult if served to guests. The porches were all different and yet the same. Most had white wicker chairs, at least one matching wicker plant stand, and one or two Adirondack chairs. Originally called Westport Chairs, Thomas Lee, who was on vacation in Westport, a small village on the shore of Lake Champlain when he designed the chairs in 1903, named them after the village. The slanted Adirondack chairs were designed to allow people to sit upright when the chairs were put on the steep hills of the Adirondack Mountains. Their wide, flat armrests were also ideal for setting a beverage or a book.

Each evening as the adults gathered to catch up on the latest big people news, the kids were left to fend for themselves. Among their favorite games were hide and seek and kick the can, especially after dark. Regardless of what they played, they knew if they misbehaved, they'd be made to sit on the porch with the grownups.

As informal meeting places, porches were the center of the neighborhood's social life. Each night the neighbors caught up with the day's activities, shared the latest news regarding their extended families, and solved most of the world's problems. Discussions about religion and politics were most common, followed by the weather and their gardens. Normally, Grant ignored adult conversations. There were, however, two major exceptions that would spike Grant's interest. The first was when the adults began spelling words instead of saying them. That was a sure give-a-way that the conversation was about something sexual. The second was the supernatural. Two or three times each summer, the conversation would turn to ghosts, unexplained occurrences, and the large hairy creatures some believed to be living in the deep woods around Benign. No one had any proof regarding the existence of these creatures, except the reports of sightings by the area farmers and hunters. Each year's fall hunting season generated another crop of stories about dead deer disappearing, isolated cabins being broken into, and reports of large, hairy man-like creatures. Grant loved such discussions and planned, if they existed, to someday track down and capture one of these creatures.

"I've gone deer hunting every year in the woods north of town near Moon Lake, where several so-called sightings have occurred, and all I've seen were hunters looking for a way to explain why they didn't bring home a deer," Stanley would eventually say toward the end of the discussion. "It's easier to tell your wife some hairy creature took your deer than it is to admit you didn't hit anything."

"That may be," Mr. Slater, Tinker's father, would always counter. "But that doesn't explain what happened to my dead deer. I've got pictures of it hanging from a tree limb and the next morning it was gone."

"Perhaps it wasn't really dead," Mrs. Lonsdale suggested.

"Even if it was alive, how do you explain it untying the knots in the rope?" Mr. Simpson asked as if it was the first time they'd had this conversation.

"Sounds more like those Wilcox brothers to me, not that those psychopaths aren't a hairy lot," Mrs. White said, looking up from her crocheting.

Meeting the Neighbors

It's a beautiful day in the neighborhood.

~Fred Rogers

The Ficks

Roger and MaryAnn Fick had sold their small dairy farm and moved into Benign after Roger injured his back. Roger took a job as a bartender at The Getman House, the second largest hotel in Jefferson County. MaryAnn, who was pregnant with their first baby, went to work as a receptionist for Dr. Baxter, who had been Benign's only doctor for longer than most memories. Roger had a hobby that never failed to entertain his porch visitors. Years earlier, in 1925, Roger's father had worked for Clinton Odell, the owner of the Burma-Shave Company. Clinton's son, Allan, had come up with an idea to stimulate sales. It was both simple and ingenious. Allan convinced his father to let him put up small, wooden roadside signs. Thinking it was a silly idea, Clinton gave his son two hundred dollars to test his signs.

At first, the signs were simple advertisements for their brushless shaving cream. The signs were an immediate success and sales soared. Over the years, as the signs spread across the country, old-fashioned wisdom, safety tips, and down-home humor became the hallmark of the Burma Shave signs. Although the white-on-red signs decorated the roadsides for years, the last new ones were put up in 1963. In the advertising war, the little white-on-red signs lost out to the huge billboards that began blocking the views along the new, faster expressways.

Roger began lining his driveway with Burma Shave signs, changing them more and more often as his collection grew. One week he would display:

My job is
Keeping faces clean
And nobody knows
De stubble I've seen"

and the next week it might be,
When Super-shave
Remember, pard
You'll still get slapped
But not so hard.

Everyone seemed to have a favorite, but the one Roger displayed most was: "
Burma-Shave
Was such a boom
They passed
The bride
And kissed the groom.

No one knew exactly how much Roger spent on his collection, only that he got them from a friend of his father who still worked for Burma Shave. However, everyone agreed that his collection would someday be worth a "pile of moolah."

The Lonsdales

The people in this neighborhood have a keen sense of rumor.

~Stanley Robinson

Gladys and Byron Lonsdale lived next door and were Grant's favorite neighbors, especially Gladys. In her seventies with no children of her own, Gladys always had a full cookie jar and plenty of cold milk for the neighborhood kids. Like all the adults in Grant's life, Gladys and Byron believed children were to be seen and not heard. When they were with their parents, Grant and Dennis were expected to stay out of everyone's hair. However, when it was just Grant and Dennis, Gladys would fall all over them with kindness. Grant especially liked Mrs. Lonsdale after she spent several afternoons teaching him how to do fifth-grade fractions.

Growing up, Grant and Dennis were taught two basic rules. The Golden Rule of doing unto others as you would have them do unto you, and "respect all adults." In addition to their parents, their grandparents, neighbors, teachers, and minister reinforced these rules. In the 1950s, nearly every aspect of a child's life was designed to teach values, responsibility, and high moral standards. Bedtime stories, movies, and radio and television shows like *Sky King*, *The Lone Ranger*, *Roy Rogers*, *Lassie*, *Gunsmoke*, and *Superman* taught children to respect authority, that good overcomes evil, and that the needs of society superseded the needs of the individual.

It was understood that, on rainy evenings, everyone would gather on the Lonsdale porch because it was the only enclosed porch in the neighborhood. The Lonsdales also had the best collection of toys to keep kids occupied and out from underfoot. They had tinker toys, silly putty, Mr. Potato Head, a pogo stick, paper dolls, different colored clay, jacks, paint by number sets, and an assortment of board games.

Virgil Thompson

There aren't many keys on Virgil's piano.

~Stanley Robinson

Virgil, a crusty old farmer, was one of Grant's favorite Benign adults, perhaps because Virgil was still a kid in the ways that mattered most. After Virgil, Grant would be forever drawn to demon-driven people. A simple man who'd never seen a building more than four stories high, Virgil never thought in terms of bigger, better, or more than. He ran a one-man, eighty-head dairy farm on the Red Lake Road, just north of the Indian Cemetery. With laugher-filled mornings, Virgil began each day expecting it to be just like the day before and the day before that. Until he was in high school, Grant thought, as everyone in Benign did, that Virgil was crazy.

Had the citizens of Benign known Latin, they would have described him as non compos mentis, Latin for, "not of sound mind." Virgil was not considered nice crazy or funny crazy, but "stay away from" crazy. Because he was single and mumbled to himself, the differing speculations about his past and lifestyle turned to rumors on their way to distrust and fear. Perhaps it was true that Virgil lost ground daily in his battle to maintain his sanity in a world he saw as an experiment gone bad, but then Grant liked people with a glint of madness in their eyes.

"Stay away from him because, if he occasionally visits reality, he doesn't stay long," Stanley told Grant and Dennis one afternoon when they'd driven by Virgil's place and noticed he'd turned his '54 Plymouth into a chicken coop on blocks and put the wheels on his hay wagon.

Virgil always smiled and waved, hoping that would be enough of a greeting. When it wasn't, his greetings varied from, "I see they finally put you to work" to "I see where the price of milk is down again" to "I see those dingbats in Washington are up to their usual tricks." Virgil liked people, but not in groups larger than one at a time. Given the way he was treated, with parents holding their kids' hands when he was around, Virgil avoided contact with most people.

"Do you know what Dichloro-Diphenyl-Trichloroethane is?" Virgil asked Grant one Saturday morning at Squealer Feeds as Grant helped him load several cans of insecticide into the back of his old pickup.

"Never heard of it."

"Don't they teach you kids nothin' at that fancy new high school of yours?"

Grant knew enough not to answer his question, nor did Virgil expect one. "Some woman named Carson wrote herself a book called *Silent Spring* and, mark my words, before long you won't be able to buy shit for killin' pests, at least not shit worth buying. That's why I'm stockin' up on this bug juice."

Grant recognized the insecticide Virgil had purchased; all ten one-gallon cans of it. Most of the farmers, including Grant's family, used it to spray their crops and to kill mosquitoes and flies. Virgil was proven right when, seven years later, Dichloro-Diphenyl-Trichloroethane (DDT) was banned in the United States and several other countries.

"Says it causes cancer ...like what the hell don't? Listen, I care about the environment as much as the next guy, but I live on the Red Lake Road with mosquitoes as big as bulldogs and twice as mean. So, Lady Carson's invertebrates, whatever the hell they are, are on their own."

"They're animals without backbones," Grant told him.

"Really? Does that include centipedes? I kind of like centipedes."

Neither of them spoke for several seconds until Virgil said, "I'm reading this other book that says people should sleep with their bodies pointing north and south so they're aligned with the earth's magnetic fields. Says it helps you sleep better, helps prevent everything from colds to rickets, and clothes you in a state of well-being."

"Do you think there's anything to it?" Grant asked.

"Maybe, but Jack Daniels will do the same thing."

The Whites

The cream of society isn't the source of the milk of human kindness.

~Stanley Robinson

Before moving to the farm in August of 1958, Grant's family rented half of a large, white, two-story house, just across the river from Squealer Feeds and a quarter-mile from Benign's business district. Their landlords, Mr. and Mrs. White, were the oldest people Grant knew, even older than his grandparents. His parents called them standoffish and Grant had heard, but didn't repeat for fear of having to hold a bar of soap in his mouth, more than one neighbor say, "Those Whites think their shit doesn't stink."

In the fifties, in Benign, nothing symbolized success and the American dream more than owning a Cadillac, and the Whites bought a new one every year. They had an AAA sticker on the back bumper of each Cadillac they owned. Grant had no idea it stood for the American Automobile Association. Rather, he thought it was some kind of grade, like getting an A in school, and it meant the Whites thought their Cadillacs were three times better than what everyone else drove.

The Whites were not only the richest and meanest people in Grant's neighborhood; they didn't like kids, especially Grant and Dennis. On any summer evening, it was common for Grant, Dennis, and the neighborhood kids to be playing hide and seek, kick the can, dodge ball, pom-pom getaway, Red Rover, or baseball in the yard in front of Stanley's side of the house, easily identifiable by the ball diamond worn into the grass. Stanley and Maretta were firm believers in their sons playing at home. "You're not traipsing all over the neighborhood," was a constant reframe.

One afternoon, Mr. White complained to Stanley about the dead grass. Stanley answered, "I'm not raising grass. I'm raising sons." Nope, there was no love lost between the Whites and the Robinsons.

Although Dennis and Grant were at the center of many arguments between their parents and the Whites, the final straw for Stanley occurred in July of 1957. After spending a week of his two-week vacation painting the White's huge two-story house (two coats), for $125.00 (half of what everyone else wanted for the job), the Whites raised the rent thirty percent saying, "The house looks so good now, we just have to raise the rent."

Three weeks later, the Robinsons moved to a small farm on the Oxbow Road. The Oxbow Road was a single-lane, poorly paved path dotted by small dairy farms. But as they road in the truck containing their family's belongings, the Oxbow Road was a wilderness trail leading Dennis and Grant to a fifty-nine-acre playground full of adventure and exploration.

Alvin Alverson

His life is made up of excesses wrapped in excuses.

~Stanley Robinson

Like Virgil, Alvin was a bachelor. Unlike Virgil, Alvin had never been married. Like Virgil, Grant's father didn't like him, often referring to him as Dipshitski. Although Alvin and Stanley both worked at St. Regis in Deferiet, they did not ride to work together. More than once Grant had heard his father say of Alvin, "He spent the first half of his life battling his way to the top and is spending the second half bottling his way to the bottom."

Alvin was a synonym for advanced simplicity. "To compensate for a lack of a viable personality, the only thing Alvin cares about is getting drunk and getting laid, usually in that order," Grant had heard his father tell his mother one Sunday afternoon. Thinking Grant was too wrapped up in reading the funnies to hear him, Stanley was telling Maretta about Alvin showing up for work drunk. Grant didn't know what "laid" meant, but he made it a point to find out.

That evening, while waiting for *Disneyland* to come on, Grant again heard his father talking in hushed tones about Alvin. He was telling Maretta about some disease Alvin had caught from "whoring around" that was "rotting his brain" and how being blind drunk all the time was causing him blackouts and flashbacks.

Grant understood whoring around was when a single man gave a single woman money to sleep with him because he didn't have a wife. What Grant couldn't understand was why the man was the one to pay or why anyone would pay someone to sleep instead of work. Hiring a woman to clean or do laundry or cook made sense, but to sleep? Grant knew there had to be more to it than that, especially if a single man could catch a brain-eating disease from sleeping with a woman.

After a glance at Grant to make sure he wasn't paying any attention to them, Grant heard his mother ask, "How can you tell when he's having a flashback?"

"If he's talking in complete sentences, he's not having one."

"But he never talks in complete sentences," Maretta replied.

"Exactly."

The Vanns: The Q Word

Your courage won't take you where it can't keep you.

~Stanley Robinson

As did most of his classmates, Grant learned about the "really cool stuff" on the playground, cool stuff being anything having to do with sex. Grant's parents weren't ones to discuss such things with their sons, at least not until a careless slip of the tongue or inappropriate behavior made it necessary for them to have one of "those talks." Grant soon learned that these talks all seemed to have something to do with making babies. However, the need for these talks would diminish drastically when Grant's parents moved the family to the farm where the cows, cats, chickens, dogs, and rabbits answered any questions the Robinson brothers had about how babies were made and born.

One sunny afternoon on the playground, Grant overheard an older kid calling Teddy Hover, one of Grant's friends, a queer. As fourth graders, neither Grant nor Teddy had a clue as to what queer meant. What they did learn that afternoon was that being a queer was bad and that queers could be identified because they wore green on Thursdays.

Grant's first mistake occurred a few days later when, while playing outside after supper, he called Dennis a queer because of his light green jacket. His second mistake was doing so within the hearing of the Whites who were sitting on their front porch at the time. A couple of minutes later, after a phone call from an indignant Mrs. White, Grant's mother appeared with what Grant's grandfather called, "The shit is about to hit the fan look." Neither of them knew which of their fans was in trouble until their mother pointed at Grant and uttered nine words all young boys dread; "Get in the house right this minute, young man."

Just inside the front door, Maretta asked, "What the hell is the matter with you? Every time I turn my back, you find another way to embarrass your father and me. You won't be happy until you've made us the laughingstock of the neighborhood." Twenty minutes after uttering the Q word, having been sent to bed early, Grant still had no idea what it met, only that using it in front of adults would generate an immediate and negative response.

The Vann twins, Kevin and Ken (called Riff and Raff by Grant's father), ruled the neighborhood "kiddom," especially the wooded area between Grant's house and the school. The Vann brothers were Benign's best-known teenage bullies and Grant's first experience with the term juvenile delinquent. Before the formation of the centralized Indian River School District, all of Benign's K-12 students were housed in the same building with the high schoolers being dismissed an hour earlier than the elementary students. Although most high schoolers played sports, had jobs, or had farm chores waiting for them at home, the Vann brothers spent their time smoking behind the Niagara Mohawk Power Relay Substation. With little else to do, their afternoon delight was terrorizing the smaller neighborhood kids as soon as they left school property.

It was a simple, unspoken arrangement. Grant would tease and insult the crap out of the Vanns and, if they caught him, they'd beat the crap out of him. A Vann beating consisted of them taking turns holding you while the other one delivering several hard punches to your upper arms. At any given time, at least one of the neighborhood boys would be sporting black and blue marks from the Vann brothers.

Having escaped a Vann ambush one afternoon, Grant made his most serious Q word mistake. From a safe distance, he called them Queers. Still not knowing what it met, he knew it would strike a nerve. Because he was within a safe running distance to his back porch, they could only yell back insults, one of which was "come over here and say that you little faggot."

Grant had no idea that queer and faggot were synonyms, but he knew faggot was no doubt another of those words you didn't say in front of adults. From that day on, Grant became the Vann brothers' favorite punching bag. Grant was no match for either of them in a fight, so he used the only two weapons he had, his sense of humor and speed. On the open ground and with a short head start, there weren't many who could catch him. The Vann brothers taught Grant that fear is faster than anger. Therefore, following his grandfather's advice of, "Never be afraid to run away from anything," Grant took great delight in making fun of the neighborhood bullies as he made a mad dash for his back porch. And because queer and faggot always generated the biggest reaction, he used both words at every opportunity. Now and then one of them would catch him, but that was a small price to pay for the sweet revenge he got when they didn't. However, with the arrival of the winter snows, Grant's courage became as tenuous as his grandfather's bladder control. When his shorter legs became his Achilles' heel, they persuaded him to seek a longer and safer route home.

The Plantz Family

Find the pattern in your mistakes.

~Stanley Robinson

"He acts like he invented sweet corn," Stanley said in describing Harold "Bud" Plantz.

"Yeah, he's the only man I know who can strut sitting down," Dirk chuckled as the two of them sat on Dirk's front pouch sipping their Pabst Blue Ribbons, doing their part to make Milwaukee famous.

Bud and Violet's family of nine was the largest in Benign. Of the seven kids (Rose, Iris, Timothy, Orchid, Barry, and Heather), Reed was the only one Grant liked playing with. What made the Plantz family even more unique was that they were all named after plants or plant parts, leading Stanley to say, "They're all a bunch of blooming idiots."

"What have they got, seven kids? Hell, they aren't even Catholic," Dirk said, irritated that anyone would have an odd number of children.

"One thing I'll give him is that he supports them without living off the public tit," Stanley murmured. "He's an honest, hardworking, family man who's not out tomcatting around. That's more than his brother-in-law can say."

Kirk chuckled. "Now there's a blooming idiot. I'm surprised he hasn't tried using his food stamps to mail his grandmother a fruit cake."

Arthur and Bertrand Wilcox

> *Luke 6:35 says love your enemies. Mark 12:31 says love your neighbors. They were talking about the same people.*
>
> ~Stanley Robinson

Everyone in Benign knew Art and Bert, the Johnson twins, who, with weathered faces locked in pain, walked through Grant's neighborhood every Saturday to get groceries and cigarettes from Clocks' Market and whiskey from The Sip and Swig, Benign's only liquor store. When it came to smoking and drinking, each was a bottle-a-day Jack Daniels downer and four-pack-a-day-Lucky Strikers. Known to the kids as the "ragged men in ragged clothes," they were purposeful drinkers and dedicated smokers, taking both vices seriously. Both alcoholics, with neither owning a car, they toted home a week's worth of food, cigarettes, and booze in two bran sacks.

Art and Bert lived about three miles from town, seldom spoke to anyone, and suffered severe lapses of hygiene. To help people tell them apart, Bert wore a sweatshirt with "Bert" painted on it in red paint. Art's shirt said, "Not Bert." Maretta, who called the Wilcox brothers "wild men from Borneo," often lectured Grant and Dennis about getting too close for fear one of them would "snatch you up and hightail it out of town." Although he heeded his mother's warning, Grant knew Shit and Shinaola, as they were called by his dad because no one could tell them apart, had all they could do to walk, let alone do any hightailing. He also knew he was never going to go to Borneo.

What a Revoltin' Development This Is!

In this country, we have baseball, football, stock-car racing, and several other real man sports instead of fencing, curling, bicycling, ice skating, and those other candy-ass, limp-wrist sports like they have in Europe.

~Brad Bodine (Mayor of Benign, 1944-1956)

Thursday, June 20, 1963 - Benign Town Council Meeting

"We don't need some damn electrically timed traffic light to tell us to stop, go, or give us permission to cross the street. I have lived here all my life and intend to continue crossing the street whenever and wherever I damn well please. I understand the need for traffic lights in cities like Watertown or Syracuse, but this is a village, not a city. That's why it says, 'Welcome to the Village of Benign' on the signs posted at the edge of town," Brad Bodine argued as the senior member of Benign's five-member town council.

Looking up from his notes, Martin Bullard, who disliked any type of confrontation, slowly took a deep breath in the hope that it would somehow refresh and fortify his waning patience. Then, looking across the table at Brad, he softly said, "Antwerp, Philadelphia, and Lafargeville are all smaller than we are and they have traffic lights. Philadelphia has three for cryin' out loud. Even Redwood, no bigger than a pimple, has a traffic light."

Martin was right about Benign's growing population. The wave of new residents began when enough baby boomer births forced growing families to move from shrinking apartments to seek the American dream of owning their own homes. Although Benign did not fit the typical concept of suburbia, it did offer what it had always offered those wishing to settle there, plenty of cheap land upon which to build a new life.

"So what, we're still called a village," Brad fired back.

"Dum-de-dum-dum," Ted Anderson, who seldom spoke at the meetings, said under his breath.

Brad, who had served three four-year terms as Benign's mayor before resigning to spend more time with his terminally ill wife, made no effort to conceal his dislike for Martin. Many on the council felt that Brad, following his wife's death, was unconsciously venting his pain and grief at Martin.

"Nevertheless, Martin has a good point," Clancy (an Irish name meaning red-headed fighter) Sheridon (an Irish name meaning wild one) said in defense of the motion on the table. "We are the fastest growing village in Northern New York and therefore we have an ever-growing number of cars passing through town. In the interest of safety and to reflect a better public image, a traffic light on the corner of Main and Commercial Streets would serve us well."

As a first-generation resident, Clancy Sheridon was still considered an outsider by native Benignians. However, to his credit, Clancy loved Benign as much as anyone and faithfully served it as a council member, a volunteer firefighter, and a member of the Benign School Board.

"We've been discussing this for almost an hour. Does anyone have anything new to add before I call for a vote?" Martin asked with a mixture of frustration and anger in his voice.

"I'd like to know if we have enough money for a traffic light?" Doris asked.

Although the only female on the testosterone-encased council, Doris Finley-Wallace had no trouble holding her own. As far as the males on the council were concerned, Doris was one of the guys. That was due, in no small measure, to her having won the Jefferson County Pipe Smoking Contest five of the last six years. She had also gone on to the State Finals, placing within the top five smokers three years running. Each contestant was given exactly one ounce of tobacco to smoke; the winner being the one who makes his or her ounce of tobacco last the longest. When defending her pipe smoking to others, Doris was quick to say, "Although women pipe smokers are now rare, female pipe smoking was very popular in the 17th and 18th centuries. Even the most respectable women smoked in public."

Brad didn't wait for Tony Rodman, the Treasurer, to respond to Doris's question. "We have more than enough money but spending it on a traffic light would be political suicide we'd live to regret."

Everyone smiled, except Brad who hadn't realize he'd made a joke. "Besides, we'd be better served if we used the money to build a chain-linked fence around the new softball diamond at Veterans Park. Not only do we have deer, Canada Geese, rabbits, dogs, and woodchucks running all over the place, Bud Stanton's cows still haven't figured out that the park isn't a pasture anymore. People are tired of taking their families to the park to find nature running amok where they want to picnic."

Ignoring Brad, Tony said, "It's everyone's civic responsibility to pay for the light. It's a taxitude. And Clancy is right about the safety aspect. Just last week I almost ran over a jaywalking tourist on Commercial Street."

"That's another damn thing we don't need," Brad replied with a scowl directed at Tony. "Every summer our streets fill up with far too many pretentious, look-down-their noses, Cadillac driving, tourists on their way to the

Thousand Islands. You can't swing a dead cat without hitting one of them, especially some young twit named Kari or Suzi or some other cutesy name ending in the letter i who's out jogging all over hell's half-acre. What's with that anyway? We have a whole generation of girls growing up with names like Debi, Terri, Wendi, and Toni. And the boys are no better, at least not those with candy-ass names like Tracy, Leslie, and Kelly. Whatever happened to names like James, Matthew, or Donald? And whatever happened to good solid nicknames like T-Bone, No-Neck Simpson, Two-By-Four Malone, and Guts-And-Nuts Malone? Say what you want, but you can trust guys with bedrock names like Colt, Rocky, and Lance."

"Those are all names of weapons," Doris commented.

"What of it? What's wrong with standup names like Turk, Stump, and Stone? Nowadays, masculine names like these are as rare as Italian Jews. Every Tom, Dick, and Harry is now named Biff."

Clancy, with a sixteen-year-old son nicknamed T.N., decided to ignore Brad's comments because he knew Brad was trying to stall the vote. It worked, much to Martin's dismay, and the meeting ended twenty minutes later when his motion was tabled for the third month in a row. Once again, Martin left a council meeting feeling like a folded hand of poker. Once again, he'd let Brad force his will upon the council and the citizens of Benign. Because Brad was a direct descendant of James and Remembrance Bodine, one of the original pioneer families who'd wrestled this part of New York away from the Iroquois in the late 1700s, he freely used his pedigree to push his own agenda.

As he walked toward his car on the far side of the parking lot, Martin couldn't help noticing Tony and Doris getting into Tony's new bright yellow Golden Hawk

Studebaker with the rear CARNUT vanity plate. Parked under the only parking lot light, Tony loved the attention he garnered from driving around town in a new car every year. Martin didn't like Doris riding with Tony because he didn't like Tony, even if he was driving her to and from the council meetings while she recuperated from a broken leg.

Martin wasn't the only one on the council who disliked Tony or at least disliked his boisterous, swaggering, self-centeredness. Of Tony, Brad often said, "If he was a rooster, he'd tell you the sun came up just to hear him crow." However, Benignians liked Tony enough to elect him to the town council for three consecutive two-year terms.

Although he was the man in the white hat and bloodstained lab coat that cut the meat "Just The Way You Want It" at Benign's Clock's One-Stop Market, Tony made extra money cutting up the area farmers' butchered steers and hogs. He also cut up deer, both in and out of hunting season with no questions asked. Now single, Tony had a well-earned reputation as a womanizer whose most prized possessions were a deer antler coat rack and a tie tack collection. Unfortunately, his womanizing hadn't ended when he married Darlene Meadows from Gouverneur, a runner-up in a Miss Dairylea Beauty Contest. Five years into their marriage, Tony was with another woman when her husband came home early. With clothes in hand, Tony jumped out a back bedroom window, twisted his ankle, and rolled down a hill into a small pond. An hour later, soaking wet and covered with cuts and bruises, Tony limped home to an irate and humiliated wife. Darlene not only knew the truth (She'd been called by the angry her husband.), she grew even more irate when Tony told her he'd been bowling and had gotten wet when someone turned on a lawn sprinkler as he took a shortcut to his car. Three months later, during their divorce proceedings, Darlene made the judge smile when she told him, "My husband lies so much that I have to call the dog for him. And as for the furniture, he can keep it. It's a bunch of junk that looks like he ordered it from a bric-a-brac catalog."

Following the council meeting, as they often did, Clancy and Martin met at The Chat-A-Wyle for a cup of coffee and one of Rosa's famous sweet rolls. Smiling at Martin, Clancy asked, "What the hell is a taxitude?"

"Beats me," Martin said as both men chuckled. "Custer knew more about fighting the Sioux than Tony knows about being treasurer." Then, on a serious note, Martin asked, "Did you know that a single Clydesdale can pull as much as 7,000 pounds but two Clydesdales, working together, can pull 25,000 pounds? I wish that just once I could get the council members to all pull in the same direction instead of our meetings being 30% posturing and 70% guerrilla warfare."

"Don't let Brad get you down. He'll come around," Clancy replied as he blew the steam off his coffee.

"I doubt it. We both know it will be a cold day in hell before he'll support anything that changes Benign. He's especially afraid that we'll end up like Alexandra Bay and become a collection of souvenir shops, ice cream stands, and antique stores."

"Then we'll have to go around him," Clancy replied with a shrug. "Most of the council agrees a traffic light is a good idea. They're just intimidated by Brad. Let me do some good old fashion arm-twisting before the next meeting."

As they toasted each other with new blue Chat-A-Wyle coffee cups, Doris was safe at home telling Brent, her husband, about the council meeting. "We did manage to get a few things done, no thanks to Brad. As usual, he was all high and mighty. Everyone's trying to be nice to him because of his wife, but patience is wearing thin."

"What bug was up his ass tonight?" Brent asked with a snarl. Brent liked people, but he made an exception for Brad. "He's like a goose, a blowhard on one end and no sense of accountability on the other."

"Don't be crude; the kids may still be awake," Doris whispered. "Did they all finish their homework?"

Brent nodded. "Marsha had some problems with her geometry. I tried to help her but it's been too long since I was in school."

"I'll look it over in the morning," Doris replied as she poured herself a cup of tea. "I was always good with figures."

"I'll say," Brent said with a glint in his eye that Doris knew all too well.

"Easy, cowboy," Doris giggled. "Don't forget I'm still a cripple."

By the time Doris had graduated from high school in the Class of '44, it was said she'd spent more time looking at ceilings than Michelangelo and that, when it came to sex, the only thing she's ever turned down was the bed. Branded a hussy, her first baby missed being conceived in wedlock by three months. Most "decent folks" had shunned her, never missing an opportunity to talk about her in hand-covered whispers. Following two husbands, three kids, and a string of hard-luck lovers, Doris distrusted any man with testicles, believing the sun had set on her dreams. However, that was before she'd met Brent Wallace.

Doris was working at the Ten Pin, the town bowling alley when she met Brent. He was new in town, drove an old jalopy, and didn't have two nickles to rub together. However, he had a great smile, did not lie, and wasn't interested in her past. Married nine years last August, Doris and Brent had a rock-solid marriage, solid enough for her to ride home in lover-boy Tony's car. Brent and Doris had found their lot in life and were busy building a future on it.

Shortly after moving to Benign, Brent got a job in the Cutter Room at St. Regis Paper Company where he and Grant's father began what would be a solid forty-year friendship. In addition to going deer hunting and ice fishing, they would often get their families together on the weekends. On Friday nights, they would watch *The Life of Riley* and *Dragnet* after Grant's family returned from their weekly A & P trip to Watertown. Occasionally, on a Saturday night, the families would get together to play board games while Brent and Stanley enjoyed *Saturday Night Boxing*. Boxing was a favorite for both men as Stanley had boxed in high school and Brent had boxed in several Golden Gloves' matches.

One of the most popular television shows in the 1950s was NBC's *The Life of Riley*. It was also one of the very first television sitcoms. Although it was a hit radio show from 1943-1951, its first television season, 1949-1950, with Jackie Gleason in the title role, didn't generate high enough ratings to keep it on the air. When it returned to television in 1953, it soon rated in the top twenty-five most-watched shows with William Bendix in the title role. Each weekly episode revolved around a different way Riley would mess up some aspect of his life. And each week the audience would wait for him to utter his signature line, "What a revoltin' development this is!"

Dragnet also had its catchphrases. Every show opened with, "This is the city, Los Angeles, California. I work here; I carry a badge." It was also famous for its, "Just the facts, ma'am" and "My name is Friday. I'm a cop." But perhaps its most famous contribution to American jargon of the '50s was the theme music, "Dum-de-dum-dum." Americans of all ages would say, "Dum-de-dum-dum," whenever they'd make a mistake that might generate negative consequences.

Bodine-isms

The pen might be mightier than the sword, but it won't cut cheese worth a shit.

The mouse doesn't give a shit about the color of the cat.

When I heard Truman won, I was happier than a teenage boy with the clap.

CHAPTER FOUR

Growing Up Down on the Farm

Benign Was More Than a Town; It Was a Time.

Benign was more than a town; it was a time when children were taught to mind their Ps and Qs, to be happy with what they had, to look for the silver lining, to lend a hand, to clean up their messes, to look after their neighbors, and to respect their elders. Children were taught to take the smallest cookie from the plate, to never take the last cookie, to look before they leaped, to think before they spoke, and that being a nurse was doing God's work. They were taught to clean their plates, not to talk with their mouths full, and not to have eyes bigger than their stomachs. They were taught money didn't grow on trees, that hard work never hurt anyone, not to put the cart before the horse, and to say please, thank you, you're welcome, and I'm sorry.

Benign was a time when children laughed at Heckle and Jeckle, Tom and Jerry, and Mighty Mouse cartoons while adults laughed at Abbott and Costello, Burns and Allen, and Jack Benny. It was a time when Vincent Price scared us with the *House of Wax, The Pit and the Pendulum,* and *The Raven*. And it was a time when the cinematic charisma of Errol Flynn entertained us with *Captain Blood, The Adventures of Robin Hood,* and *Santa Fe Trail*.

Benign was a time of snipe hunts, frozen clothes on the line, rabbit ears with tinfoil, elephant jokes, and tail fins on cars. It was a time of phone booth packing, *TV Guide*, mohair sweaters, dashboard hula girls, Perry Mason, the Brooklyn Dodgers, 18 cent a gallon gas, Dick Tracy, flagpole sitting, Dobie Gillis, mood rings, the Amazing Kreskin, Aquaman, pea shooters, Zagnut candy bars, Evil Knievel, draft notices, *Laugh-in*, Dickies, Dick and Jane, Lawrence Welk, Ozzie and Harriet, doctors making house calls, and Necco candy wafers.

The Second Chance - Saturday, March 25, 2006

"Did you ever go to a sock-hop?"

"Just one, that time we were snowed in at the high school so they put everyone in the gym," Grant answered.

"I remember spending that night dancing with Brenda. I had a huge crush on her for a while. She could make an hour seem like a minute and a minute last forever."

"I think you and every other boy in school had the hots for her. Well, everyone except me," Grant grinned. "I was so busy digging those rhythms and blues with Cindy that night that I don't remember much else, except, like in McLean's song, kicking off our shoes and dancing in the gym. With her head on my shoulder, the sweet smell of her soft hair, and my hand on the small of her back, I could have died happy, then and there, in the knowledge that nothing would ever be better than it was at that moment."

"Cindy now lives on High Street with her husband and too many cats to count. Having made the most of her Wonder Years, she wears aging well and still looks good enough to remind me of the sound of vows breaking," T.N. grinned. "But I know how you felt dancing with her. The lines about feeling her touch, the warmth of her embrace, and being in heaven in Bobby Helms's 1957 hit, "My Special Angel," was a perfect description of how I felt while dancing with Brenda."

"I don't remember; did you and Brenda ever go steady?"

"I sure wanted to, but I'm afraid I was more of an average Joe than a Romeo. We went on a couple of dates, where she tried putting me down several times and would have had she found a vet."

Smiling, Grant replied, "As I recall, many of your dates were described in affidavits."

"Yeah, you know you're going to have a great date or a really bad date when the girl slams you against the wall and asks if you have a safe word. The problem was that I wanted to reap a hell of a lot more than Brenda wanted to sow," T.N. grinned. "She had virtues I liked and vices I loved. And she always brought protection on our dates; unfortunately, it was a switchblade in her purse."

They both laughed.

"Brenda and I never hit it off. She regarded me with an indifference bordering on aversion, at least until our senior year when we managed to forge a truce," Grant reflected.

T.N. blew on his hot coffee before he resumed his interpretation of McLean's song. "The pickup truck has long been a symbol of the macho, independent male, especially if the driver is wearing western boots and hat. Perhaps it's that macho "bronckin' buck" image McLean was referring to when he wrote about a teenager bronckin' buck, a pink carnation, and a pickup truck."

Grant nodded. "Is the pink carnation a reference to the song, "A White Sport Coat and a Pink Carnation?"

"I think so. "A White Sport Coat and a Pink Carnation" by Martin Robinson was the number one Country song in 1957."

"Who was Martin Robinson?"

"He's better known as Marty Robbins," T.N. replied before again blowing across the top of his coffee cup.

Guilt Filled Silence

> *I'm not as bad as the worst things I've done or as good as the best things I've done.*

Grant and Dennis were raised on farm food, knew how to work from dawn to dusk, and understood what "traipsing all over hell's half-acre" meant. As they drove through Benign and then onto the Oxbow Road, Grant felt like a salmon returning home, returning to his roots, returning to the beginning before the beginning. It had been Dennis's idea to celebrate his retirement by taking Grant back to the farm. Dennis graduated high school with Karen, who'd purchased the farm from Grant's parents. Dennis had gotten Karen's permission for them to come back to wander around in their memories.

In 1964, the times weren't only changing, they were confusing to a sixteen-year-old farm kid living in a little white house on a narrow strip of blacktop connecting nowhere to everywhere. Two miles from town, Grant believed the word farm came from a Latin word meaning, "I've got to get the hell out of here." However, in August of 1957, as Dennis and Grant rode in the truck containing their family's belongings, the Oxbow Road was a wilderness trail leading them to a fifty-nine-acre playground with miles of elbowroom in every direction. Today, to his surprise (and disappointment), Grant would discover the Oxbow Road had become a paved, two-lane road with quarter-million-dollar homes replacing most of the farmhouses of his youth. Benign had been discovered by well-heeled city types seeking the peace and quiet of country living.

Saturday, June 2, 2007, was sunny and warm, with just a hint of a breeze as Grant and Dennis walked around the outbuildings, roamed through the woods, and wandered across the meadows. The highlight was Karen's tour of the house. Although she'd remodeled it, including converting the basement into a family room, it was still the keeper of Dennis and Grant's memories; memories that came flooding out of the walls that had held them sacrosanct for over fifty years.

That night, as sleep eluded him, Grant replayed his memories of his first night and second day as a farm kid. Stanley bought it for $3,500, a fair price in 1957, and moved them into it the summer before Grant entered the sixth grade. Combined with the excitement of being in a new house with its unfamiliar creaks and moans, the croaking frogs kept Grant awake well past midnight. From the racket, Grant knew there had to be at least a thousand of them in the small swamp at the bottom of the hill near their new property line. He decided he'd go frog hunting the next morning.

Armed with a hearty breakfast and a pocket full of rocks, Grant led an expedition (Dennis) into Croaker Swamp. They named it that because swamps need a name to make them sound more dangerous. However, they weren't very successful, killing fewer than a half-dozen frogs. Discouraged, they returned home believing the frogs they'd heard the night before, and now couldn't find, must be night croakers. They named them that to make them sound more dangerous.

Although still excited about sleeping in the new house, Grant laid awake that second night listening to the silence from Croaker Swamp. Not a single frog could be heard croaking, teaching Grant that there's nothing louder than silence filled with guilt. The silence from Croaker Swamp also taught Grant not to confuse the loud croaking by others with what he knew to be right.

Grownups Have Some Funny Ideas

Finding trouble has never been much of a challenge.

~Meredith LoBello

Grant sat quietly on what he'd later come to call the Group W Bench, just inside the Principal's Office, trying to feel sad and look innocent at the same time. Head down, Grant knew how to look in an adult's eyes long enough to express repentance, but not long enough to look combative or defiant. The Group W Bench, a name Grant took from Arlo Guthrie's song, "Alice's Restaurant", was where the troublemakers and rule-breakers sat to cool their heels before being taken behind the large counter and into Mr. Fields's private office.

A few minutes later, Mr. Fields came for Grant, escorted him around the counter, and told him to take a seat in one of the chairs facing his desk. It wasn't a long interrogation, and, to Grant's surprise, Mr. Fields didn't seem interested in punishing him. Grant explained that several of the boys were playing softball during recess, that Don Hunter had hit a long drive into center field, and that Harley Brown, who wasn't playing on either team, picked it up and ran off with it.

"And then?"

"And then I ran after her to get our ball back and when she wouldn't give it to me I took it away from her."

"She says you hit her in the stomach. Is that true?"

Grant nodded yes without saying anything. He wasn't about to tell the principal that the only way he could get a girl, especially one smaller than him, to drop the ball was to punch her in the stomach. Nor did he tell Mr. Fields that after she recovered, she chased him halfway across the playground. Harley might have been stronger and a better fighter than Grant, but she wasn't much of a runner. Then, unable to catch him, she squealed to the playground aide.

"I think we need to discuss why you can't go around punching girls in the stomach," Mr. Fields said as he got up to close the door. Returning, he sat on the edge of his desk, looking down at Grant. In a silky-smooth voice, Mr. Fields explained that hitting girls in the stomach was different than hitting boys because you might hurt the girls so they couldn't have babies when they grew up.

Grant had lived on the farm long enough to know that babies didn't come from a mother's stomach. He must have looked confused because Mr. Fields said, "I know all of this is new to you. I've talked to your mother and she and your dad will answer all your questions tonight." Grant left the principal's office thinking Mr. Fields had some weird ideas and that perhaps he should be the one to talk to his parents. It was only common sense to Grant that, if babies came from women's stomachs, that they'd have to give birth by throwing up.

A Bolt from the Blue

Teaching isn't the filling of vessels, but the lighting of fires.

~Bruce Nieuwenhuis

The realization that he'd eventually grow into a schoolteacher came to Grant, as his grandmother often said, "like a bolt from the blue." Without warning, an eleven-year-old Grant heard himself whisper, "I'm going to be a teacher." Not, "I'd like to be a teacher," or "I want to be a teacher," but "I'm going to be a teacher." As far as Grant was concerned, it was a done deal written in stone. So shocked by it, Grant can still remember the exact moment it occurred.

On Wednesday afternoon, November 27, 1957, the day before their Thanksgiving holiday, Mr. Borcey, Grant's sixth-grade teacher, poured a small beaker of water into an empty, one-gallon maple syrup can. He then placed the can over a Bunsen burner until the water in the can began to boil. Then he placed the can on a nearby hot pad, quickly screwed on the top, and asked, "What's going to happen?"

None knew the correct answer, nor were any of them prepared for the shock of seeing the can slowly buckle as if a large, invisible foot was stepping on it. As amazed as he was by the experiment, Grant was far more impressed with how his classmates responded in glee. At that moment, Grant knew he wanted to spend his life generating that kind of awe and wonder in students of his own. Although he would briefly consider other occupational options, (law enforcement, a marine biologist, the ministry, and a veterinarian), it was an imploding Maple Syrup can that revealed Grant's destiny.

Anne Lamb, one of Grant's favorite authors, wrote, "Many sculptors report they can see the finished work already existing within the stone. All they do is remove the extra stone. What we want to become already exists within us. Our growth isn't a matter of what we need to add, but a matter of what we need to remove. I suspect Albert Einstein was correct when he said, 'The important thing is to never stop questioning' and I also suspect a question is our best tool for chipping away at the extra stone in our lives."

Rosa-isms

Most of us are two people, our own best friend and our own worst enemy.

Wrestling with your conscience is like wrestling a gorilla. You don't stop until the gorilla stops.

Trouble with Troopers

> *Yo-yo is a Tagalog word (Tagalog is the native language of the Philippines.) and means to come back. Donald Duncan, the man most responsible for the yo-yo becoming popular in North America, was not its inventor. Records of its use date back twenty-five centuries. After the doll, it is the world's oldest toy and was the first toy taken into space. It was introduced in the United States in the 1860s but was not mass-produced until the 1920s. Sales grew steadily over the years, reaching their peak in 1962 when forty-five million were sold. Donald Duncan also marketed the first parking meters.*

Better than any eleven-year-old had a right to be, Ray Duncan basked in his classmates' awe and envy at his arm walker, boomerang, rock the baby, and around the world. No one can remember if they'd tagged him "Yo-yo" because of his skill or because his last name was the same as their favorite brand of yo-yos. They'd nicknamed James, the other half of the Duncan brothers, JD. With only a year separating them, they were each other's best friends. Both were bright, friendly, and easygoing. In choosing sides, one was always chosen first and the other last. One was thin with bright red hair; the other was a moderately overweight toe head.

Although it was mid-January, the roads were plowed and salted bare. Yo-yo loved his music loud and lean and his speed always exceeded whatever the law allowed. They were well over the posted limit and leaning into the turns when Yo-yo was pulled over by a New York State Trooper. In the first of what would become several visits to the backseats of police cars, Grant sat quietly listening to the trooper's lecture as he wrote up Yo-yo's well-deserved ticket. The silver-gray box displaying 66 on the front seat had silenced any denial Yo-yo had been formulating as the Trooper walked them to his patrol car.

From the front seat, Yo-yo had a better view of the trooper when he left them alone to kick the snow off Yo-yo's back license plate. Returning to the patrol car, the trooper continued his lecture about keeping license plates free of ice and snow as he completed the ticket. After several assurances that it wouldn't happen again that included an adequate number of, "Yes officer," and "No officer," they were finally free to go with the ticket in hand. Ten minutes down the road, Yo-yo pulled a pair of leather gloves from his coat pocket and giggled, "How long do you think it will take him before he misses these?"

Years earlier, as another gray uniformed state trooper and Grant's father stood talking on the front porch, Grant had concentrated on looking innocent. Although he couldn't hear what they were saying, he knew what they were discussing. When Stanley called him over, Grant took a deep breath and let it out slowly, hoping the escaping air would somehow suck the butterflies from his belly. Buried beneath the gaze of two pairs of soul-searching eyes, Grant made two important decisions. First, he'd lie. Second, regardless of the evidence against him, he'd stick to the lie. Grant had long known that not cracking under pressure was critical in preventing the light from entering.

The trooper began with questions Grant could easily answer truthfully. Yes, he knew James Duncan. Yes, he often went to James's house after school. Yes, Grant knew about the old barn near the river. And yes, he and James often played there. With each truthful response, Grant was gaining the confidence he'd need when he'd exhausted his supply of honesty. It didn't take long. No, Grant hadn't noticed any broken windows. No, he didn't know how they came to be broken or who might have broken them. And, most important, Grant didn't break them. He was so convincing he almost believed he was innocent. Then, pushing his luck, Grant expanded on the truth by volunteering that he and James had played there three days before and he hadn't noticed any broken windows. Grant didn't know if it was instinct or if some lying gene had kicked in, but he knew that freely admitting he was there while insisting the windows were not broken sounded more credible than simply denying any involvement.

Then the trooper caught him off guard when he said that James had already admitted his guilt and had squealed on Grant as well. It was a well-sprung trap and Grant could feel his father's eyes listening for his response. By the seventh grade, Grant already had a well-developed mistrust of authority, and standing in front of him was over six feet of pure authority with a gun on his hip. The trooper looked credible, but how could Grant be sure he wasn't bluffing? Grant went with the cards he'd dealt himself and stuck to his story. Looking directly at the Trooper, he innocently said something like, "I don't know why he'd say that. I was with him the entire time and I didn't see him break any windows."

The point, counterpoint, the bluff had been called. The trooper was good. He did not say anything, letting the silence pile up on itself. During the forever they looked at each other, the trooper's eyes were swords while Grant's were shields. Grant knew intuitively that the first one to speak had lost. Finally, the trooper closed his notebook and thanked Stanley and Grant for their assistance. However, Stanley wasn't so easily bluffed. Stanley's silence said even more than his expression as he slowly turned and left his son standing alone outside the screen door. Grant learned in school the next morning that James had broken under the pressure and had spilled the truth all over the trooper. For the next several weeks, James's allowance went to repay his parents the cost of replacing the broken windows while Grant escaped having to accept any responsibility for his actions.

Actions can lie louder than words.

Avoid those who, when they are going under, shed their principles.

When the tough get going, someone is going to get screwed.

Growing Up Down on the Farm

A cow is an appetite covered with hide.

Every Saturday during the winter my father and I would struggle to keep warm while cutting down trees for our family's fuel supply. We didn't own a chain saw so we used a crosscut saw consisting of a long blade with a wooden handle on each end. My end of the saw taught me many lessons, including how to wait my turn, when to push, and when to pull. I learned pulling doesn't always get me what I want, that pushing isn't giving, and that giving is often allowing someone else to pull. We had a black and white mutt named Lucky. A tree we were downing fell on him and, although he wasn't hurt, I learned not to put faith in names because there are also forces at work within the universe that do not respect symbolism.

Growing up on a farm also offered a wide variety of life lessons. Now, fifty years after leaving the farm, I more fully appreciate the expression, "You can take the boy out of the country, but you can't take the country out of the boy." Here are some of the lessons I carried from the farm.

If an animal bites you a second time, you deserve it.

When a dog shares food with a cat, it's the cat's food.

It takes more hot water to warm cold water than it takes cold water to cool hot water.

Your own chores are the hardest until you have to do someone else's.

The tastiest apples grow on the smallest limbs at the top of someone else's tree.

Country fences are for keeping in while city fences are for keeping out.

No matter how long an animal lives, the length of time it's dead is always the same.

To protect the cat from the dog, hold the dog, not the cat.

It's better to get wind of it before you're standing in it.

Off the farm, the clock tells you when the job is done. On the farm, the job tells you when you're done.

The horse is complete without the rider.

The loudness of a frog's croaking tells you nothing about the length of its jump.

The moon is not discouraged, distracted, or diverted by howling dogs.

Don't hang your coat on someone else's nail.

Snakes aren't that long if you don't count the tail.

Don't trust anyone your dog doesn't like.

Treat the earth with respect, kindness, and gentleness; she's pregnant.

Still water freezes first.

Learn to listen. There is a big difference between ground hog meat and groundhog meat.

The best way of not getting the bent fork is to set the table.

God gave us dogs to teach us about loyalty and cats to teach us that not everything serves a purpose.

Chickens look at you sideways, cows look past you, dogs look up to you, cats look down on you, but pigs look you in the eye and accept you as an equal.

Huffing and Puffing
smoked, v. cured by exposing to smoke

It was all around them, so close and yet so far. There were glimpses of it everywhere, mostly in the shadows and whispered promises of pleasures to come. Grant and Dennis viewed aging as an admit one ticket to adulthood, that secret world of sex, cigarettes, dirty jokes, beer, and all the other fun stuff they were told they were too young to understand. To them, adulthood was a treasure trunk of privileges and behaviors that were only considered sins if you were a kid. Therefore, a large quantity of their time was devoted to finding ways of secretly sampling the trunk's contents.

Eventually, they figured out how to cross that mystical threshold, if only in a small way. It was a great plan based upon the false assumption that all smoke looks and smells alike. They planned and prepared for over a week while collecting cigarette butts from ashtrays and hiding them in an old Del Monte Stewed Tomato can in the milk house. Everything went smoothly and by mid-week, they knew the guardians of adulthood's gates were with them when a snowstorm left four-foot drifts around their burning barrel.

While Grant was growing up, every farm had a burning barrel and its own dump. The Robinson burning barrel was a fifty-gallon drum Stanley had brought home from the paper mill where he worked full-time. Stanley also worked full-time farming Hungry Hill, fifty-nine acres that absorbed all his time, money, and energy. One of Grant's Saturday morning chores was to burn the previous week's papers. Located a few yards from the house, it took about six months' worth of ashes to fill the barrel enough for it to be taken to the dump. Their dump was at the bottom of a cliff about a quarter of a mile behind the barn. In addition to burning barrels, their dump also accepted weekly donations of any other debris generated on their small farm.

Following a week of exchanging knowing smiles, Grant and Dennis were ready. After setting fire to the papers, they hid behind the barrel and snowdrifts to light up; confident their cigarette smoke would blend in with the paper smoke. It was their first smoking experience and their first attempt at grownup "coolness" as their fiery throats fought to purge their lungs in dragon-like breaths. Despite the discomfort, they exchanged knowing smiles as they watched the cigarette smoke lazily twist and turn in the rising currents like murky lullabies. Stanley never explained how he knew what they'd done, deepening their belief in the mystical powers of parenthood. As they returned to the house, confident they'd successfully trespassed upon alien soil, Stanley confronted them with what promised to be a very long lecture. Then, with a knowing smile, his mood abruptly changed as he christened them citizens in the world of smoking, slapped them on the back, and told them to have a seat while he went to get something with which to celebrate their newfound status. They couldn't believe their good fortune as they sat exchanging knowing smiles on the family couch. Grant can remember telling Dennis how cool they'd be in school when their friends learned their dad thought they were old enough to smoke.

Knowing that a valid argument seldom comes wrapped in a shout, Stanley showed far less anger than he felt as he produced three caustic cigars and lead his sons down that mystery encrusted hallway to adulthood. The three laughed, puffed, boasted, and bonded beneath the knowing smiles Stanley and Maretta exchanged as she occasionally surveyed them from the kitchen doorway.

After finishing their cigars, Stanley insisted they continue their celebration by having a slice of hot cherry pie Maretta had just taken from the oven. Then, as they finished the pie, the pie finished Grant. It was while throwing up in the newfound knowledge that knowing smiles often conceal more than they reveal, that Grant learned that life's journey is most often down a toll road. Not Dennis. Proceeding with manly intent, he downed the second slice of cherry pie. Years later, Dennis became an avid smoker. However, Grant had learned his father's lesson well. Although it's been over fifty years, Grant hasn't yet eaten another piece of cherry pie.

Dennis-isms

After reading how bad smoking is, I immediately quit reading.

I'm a vegetarian, not because I love animals, but because I hate plants.

Kelsey's Bull

> *As you know, we don't have relationships with Iran. I mean, that's — ever since the late '70s, we have no contacts with them, and we've totally sanctioned them. In other words, there's no sanctions — you can't — we're out of sanctions.*
>
> ~George W. Bush

    The only thing between the large white bull and my baby sister was Duke, our German Shepherd. I didn't see it, but the entire episode is firmly fixed in our family's oral history as the day Duke saved Kathy's life. According to the story, Kelsey's bull had broken through the fence and was running wild in our backyard. Then, as it came around to the front of the house and saw two-year-old Kathy playing on a blanket, it charged. Duke, seeing the danger, risked his safety by attacking the bull. He repeatedly prevented the bull from harming Kathy until my mother heard the commotion and rescued her. Just how much of the story is true has been lost in the telling and retelling, but the rest of the story is as accurate as I can remember.

    The bull was still running around our yard when my father, brother, and I returned from Squealer Feeds. After hearing what had happened, my father lost his temper as he found the phone. He insisted Kelsey come get his bull, but Kelsey refused saying he was too busy and would get it later. Now angrier, my father hung up and ordered us to stay in the house as he unsuccessfully attempted to drive the bull off with a pitchfork. A few minutes later my father again called Kelsey who again refused, saying he was busy painting his kitchen. My father hung up and smiled at me as he said, "Kelsey is more focused upon my anger than the problem. I'll wait a few minutes until he calms down and then I'll make our problem his problem so he'll focus upon a solution." A few minutes later, in a quiet, calm voice, my father again called Kelsey, asking him to listen carefully as he placed a deer rifle next to the phone and loaded a shell into the chamber. Before hanging up, he told Kelsey he had exactly five minutes to come to get his bull or he'd shoot it.

I had long since learned that "say it, mean it, do it" was more than a saying to my father and there wasn't a doubt in my mind that my father would kill the bull. Kelsey also believed it because he was in our yard well within five minutes. Although he and my father exchanged some angry words, the bull offered no resistance as Kelsey slipped on the halter, tied it to the back of his truck, and slowly drove out of our yard. Returning his rifle to the pegs over the bookcase, my father said, "Ben Franklin was right. If you get them by the balls, their hearts and minds will follow." I don't know if Ben Franklin actually said that, but I do know why most people believed my father was sired by a flash of lightning.

Stanley-isms

Don't take the bull by the tail unless you're also willing to take it by the horn.

If you take the bull by the horns, you've had some really bad advice.

CHAPTER FIVE

Rough Road To Romance

Benign Was More Than a Town; It Was a Time.

Benign was a time when civility was the norm when your neighbors were as honest as the day is long, when holding public office was a privilege, and when the fewer people had the more they shared. It was a time when going to sleep to a tin-roof rain was as good as it got. Benign was a time when taking care of the sick, widows, and orphans was everyone's responsibility and not that of some governmental agencies.

Benign was more than a town; it was a time when everyone was in the same boat, and everybody rowed. It was a time when children did their chores, not for an allowance, but because being a member of a family came with shared responsibilities. Benign was watermelon stands, Eskimo pies, donkey basketball games, *Weekly Readers*, playing marbles, air raid drills, "Kilroy was here," soda jerks, Mercurochrome, "Railroad crossing, look out for the cars," Captain Midnight Rings, Lava Soap, fly strips, aluminum siding salesmen, 20 Mule Team Borax, x-ray machines in shoe stores, spittoons (cuspidors), and cars before "blinker lights."

Benign was a time when Sophia Loren, Jane Russell, Ava Gardner, Jane Mansfield, Gina Lollabridgida, Brigette Bardot, and Marilyn Monroe set the beauty standard by which all women, fairly or not, were judged. It was a time when Walter Cronkite was "the most trusted man in America" and Roman Catholic services were in Latin.

Benign was a time of Dick and Jane watching Spot run, letter sweaters, Future Farmers of America in their blue jackets, beatniks, and pregnant was being in a family way.

Saturday, March 25, 2006 - The Second Chance

"Did your parents ever say, 'A rolling stone gathers no moss?'"

"Sure, all the time," Grant replied, smiling at the memory of his grandmother sitting in her stuffed chair dishing out her pronouncements like a queen on high.

T.N. held up his coffee cup as he caught April's (the current owner of The Second Chance) eye. Then, turning back to Grant, T.N. said, "I think McLean revised that expression to moss growing fat on a rolling stone to make a statement about Bob Dylan."

"I thought he was talking about the Rolling Stones."

"That may very well be right. But I tend to go with those thinking he's referring to Dylan because 'Like a Rolling Stone' was Dylan's first hit. In that song Dylan described himself as being without a home and a complete unknown, because he rarely gave straight answers when interviewed, wanting to be 'a complete unknown' by telling several different stories about his past."

"I can't believe it," April said as she approached their booth with a fresh pot of coffee. "The two of you haven't seen each other in coon's age and you're spending your time talking about some old folk singer."

T.N. and Grant looked at each other and laughed out loud.

"You ever listen to Dylan?" Grant asked.

"My father loves him, but I like songs I can understand," April teased. "Besides, he mumbles too much for me."

As April walked away, T.N. tore open a bag of Splenda for his coffee before saying, "Just like back in high school, no one we knew liked Dylan."

"There were a few. Besides my brother and his friend

Don Smith, Cindy was deep into Dylan."

T.N. nodded, pleased there'd been others from Benign whose musical interests went beyond Elvis and the Beatles. "After Dylan released 'Like A Rolling Stone,' he disappeared for several years. Many believe Dylan is being described as a rolling stone in the song because he spent those years sitting around growing fat on all his royalty checks."

"Then the rest of the verse would also be about Dylan, making him the jester."

"That's right. Dylan was nicknamed Jester in the '60s because so many of his lyrics were both political and symbolic riddles, like the jesters of old who entertained kings and queens. Secondly, shortly after President Kennedy's assassination, Jackie described him and his presidency by quoting from the musical *Camelot*."

"*Don't let it be forgot, that for one brief, shining moment, there was Camelot,*" Grant said, glad he could add a little to the conversation.

"After that, Jack and Jackie were nicknamed the King and Queen of Camelot. The line about the Jester singing for the King and Queen probably refers to Dylan singing for the Kennedys during the March on Washington. Then again, many believe the king and queen refer to Bobby Darin and Connie Francis dating in the late fifties, and still, others think it's a reference to Elvis being the King."

"Dylan is often described as being the voice of our generation so the lyric about a voice coming from you and me probably refers to him speaking for us baby boomers."

How does the line about him borrowing a coat from James Dean fit into all of this?"

"Ah, you'll love this. In *Rebel Without a Cause*, Dean wore a windbreaker that he lends to a guy who is later killed. Immediately after the movie was released, that and similar windbreakers sold out across the country. Do you remember the cover on Dylan's 'The Freewheelin' Bob Dylan' album?"

"Yeah, he's walking down the street with a young woman."

"In that picture, the windbreaker he's wearing is almost identical to the one Dean wore in the movie."

The Cost of Breaking the Rules

Don't let failure go to your head.

In 1957, Tang went on sale, *The Music Man* and *West Side Story* opened on Broadway, the *Cat in the Hat* was published, Velcro was patented, and thirteen-year-old Bobby Fischer became a chess champion. The Civil Rights Act of 1957 became law, the word beatnik was introduced, *Have Gun Will Travel* came to television, and John F. Kennedy earned a Pulitzer for his *Profiles in Courage*.

In 1957, she had a hydrogen-brazed, dip-tube streamlined frame, *a frame that sucked the very breath from Grant's body every time he saw her. At $62.95, Grant could only dream of her.* She had a black enamel finish with red trim, gold pinstripes, gold and white decals, bright chrome plated parts, and, *in her poodle skirt, she was the most beautiful thing he'd ever seen.* She had chrome-plated rims, Allstate Deluxe balloon whitewalls, and, at less than seventy pounds, *she seemed to float through the air.* She was the J. C. Higgins Deluxe Bicycle, manufactured by Sears, Roebuck, and Company, and *answered, "Present," every morning when Mr. Borcey took attendance.* Grant didn't question the strange desires and longings her presence generated; much like the desires, stirrings, and longings, he felt toward the new J. C. Higgins. However, Grant was soon spending far less time thinking about a new bicycle and far more time dreaming about Cindy and him walking in tandem. Cute as a bug, Cindy would introduce Grant to several emotions that year, the two strongest of which were love and jealousy. By the time Fats Domino released his hit song, "I Want to Walk You Home," in 1959, Grant had walked Cindy home at least a thousand times, but only at the core of his wishful thinking.

Grant tried his best to become the center of Cindy's attention without a whiff of success. He wrote her notes she didn't answer, teased her without ever generating a smile, and sought to learn as much as he could about her. That Christmas, Grant drew a girl's name for the Secret Santa gift exchange. Although everyone was to keep their names secret, it didn't take Grant long to ferret out who had Cindy's name. "Wouldn't you know it?" Grant murmured at learning Jim Cummings, the class heartthrob, had drawn Cindy's name. Jim refused to trade names with Grant, mostly because he was afraid to break the rules. Grant didn't suffer under any such notions and breaking a couple of silly rules, including bribery, to get his love's name was a minor detail to him. It took Grant an hour of weeding Mrs. Lonsdale's flower garden to earn the ten cents Jim demanded before he'd trade names with him. The deal was consummated during recess with Grant going home that day with Cindy's name on a small, folded slip of paper.

Grant's first lesson in the perils of love came a couple of days later when Mr. Borcey found out about the trade and made Grant and Jim trade back to their original names. However, he refused Grant's request that Jim also should return the dime. Instead of losing recess, staying after school, or taking a note home to his parents, Mr. Borcey told Grant the loss of his dime was the price he'd have to pay for breaking the rules. Grant's argument that Jim was then making a profit from breaking the same rules was logic Mr. Borcey seemed unable to grasp. This "selective rule enforcement" only served to deepen Grant's distrust of authority. Mr. Borcey's lesson was lost on Grant because he didn't give a damn about the dime or the rules he'd broken. To him, losing the dime was better than the other punishments he could have gotten and, therefore, a cheap price to pay. It also reinforced a philosophy Grant was learning to live by: if you don't mind doing the time, do the crime. Although Grant was knee-deep in love with Cindy and sinking fast, she spent the remainder of that year treating Grant as a minor irritation, like a persistent fly at a picnic.

Grant wasn't one to start a fist fight, at least not until he discovered that Ray Duncan, a friend, and classmate, also liked Cindy and heard the negative whispers of the green-eyed monster shouting in his ear. Somewhere in the back of his mind, Grant knew he couldn't defeat Ray, but his jealousy had pushed everything else aside. On the way home after school, Grant confronted Ray, telling him to, "Stay away from Cindy." Words quickly turned to shoves on their way to exchanged punches. The fight didn't last long, mostly because Pat Kelly, a Benign storeowner, broke it up, saving Grant from certain defeat. Grant, because his anger had dulled the pain of Ray's blows, felt he'd made his point. The only good news coming out of the fight was Grant later learning that Cindy didn't like either of them.

When their sixth-grade class moved on to junior high the following year, Grant and Cindy were in different classes. Nothing had changed between them; Grant was still in love with her while she gave him looks that felt like a cold shower. However, what Grant lacked in style and substance he made up for in persistence. He was again writing her notes, following her around like a lovesick puppy, and hoping against hope she'd go with him. A top student with a keen mind and a stinging wit, both she and Grant knew she was out of his league. She agreed to let him walk her home one night and Grant was sure she could hear his heart pounding. When they arrived, Cindy insisted they stand out of sight of her mother who they could see through the kitchen window. With trembling lips and shaky legs, Grant asked Cindy to go steady with him. After refusing (twice), Grant watched her turn and walk up the hill toward home without looking back.

Although their lockers were next to each other, Cindy and Grant didn't speak the next morning. Grant wanted to say something to her, but what? He'd asked and she'd answered, so what was there to talk about? If Cindy wouldn't go with him, he couldn't stop her. Besides, Grant was drowning in embarrassment and had all he could do to face her, let alone come up with enough words to form a sentence. However, that afternoon one of Cindy's friends told Grant that Cindy did like him, that she didn't want him to be angry with her, and that she'd said no because her parents wouldn't allow her to go steady. As they met at their lockers at dismissal that afternoon, Cindy, with a smile Grant could almost taste, in a voice barely above a whisper, said, "Hi there." Immediately, those two words erased the previous night's embarrassment, and her warm, puppy-dog look dissolved the day's humiliation. With his tongue stuck to the back of his teeth, Grant barely managed to return her greeting before he lost his ability to form words as each syllable glued itself to the roof of his mouth.

Grudges grow heavier by the day.

How you interpret, interprets you.

Memories Are Made of This

No mom, I wasn't kissing Cindy. I was just whispering into her mouth.

Tuesday, January 15, 1963 – Bus #9

After school, that day, the high school Science Club went on a field trip to Dry Hill, an area Radar Defense Station. The bus driver, as luck would have it, was Sam, the driver on Grant's regular bus route. Sam liked Grant because Grant enjoyed sitting behind him listening to his war stories on the drive home. Sam had driven the high school runs long enough to recognize young love when he saw it. Taking Grant aside he asked, "How about I take the Ore Bed Road on the way home tonight?"

Grant smiled as he nodded. Taking Grant home first instead of going directly into Benign would add a good twenty minutes to the amount of time he'd spend with Cindy. And for extra measure, Sam turned off all the interior lights. Grant's perfect night was about to get better.

Grant had been looking for an opportunity all evening, and it finally came as Sam stopped the bus at the bottom of the hill in front of Grant's house. They'd been sitting with his arm around her and, before the lights came on at his stop, Grant leaned toward her for their first kiss. Grant had heard about "kisses sweeter than wine," but nothing had prepared him for the hot sweetness of Cindy's moist lips. Nor did he know which thrilled him more, him kissing her or her kissing back. Melting against him, Cindy made no pretense about wanting to kiss as much as he did as she eagerly met him halfway. Grant would have other girlfriends and other first kisses but, until he met Joan, none of them were as sweet as that kiss on the best night of his first sixteen years.

That following Saturday afternoon, with his chores done, Maretta dropped Grant off at The Chat-A-Wyle on her way to her bowling league match. Grant loved to read at the diner as he sipped a cream soda and listened to the latest jukebox tunes. "How was that field trip?" Rosa asked as Grant claimed the last stool at the end of the eight-stool counter.

"Great," Grant beamed.

"Did Cindy go?"

"Yeah," Grant said with a mile-wide smile.

"So, did you finally kiss her?" Rosa asked after making sure no one was close enough to hear her.

Grant nodded as he felt the red moving upward from his neck to warm his ears. Although he felt uncomfortable talking to an adult about his first real girl kiss, Rosa wasn't like other adults. Grant knew his mom would be fine with him having a girlfriend, especially if it were Cindy, but if Cindy's mom found out, they'd both be DOA. Cindy's mom didn't hold Grant in as high esteem as Maretta held Cindy. A few days later, when she learned Grant and Cindy were "an item", Maretta was especially pleased that her eldest had picked a Catholic girl, just like his father had done.

"About time," Rosa whispered. Then, still teasing him, she said, "She's a really sweet girl, far too sweet for the likes of you. So, tell me, how did kissing her make you feel?"

Grant took several thoughtful seconds before he slowly replied, "Like I was homesick for someplace I've never been." Then, leaning forward across the counter, Grant softly said, "She kissed me with her eyes closed, so I closed mine. Why do people close their eyes when they kiss?"

Rosa laughed aloud. "Perhaps closing our eyes is a subconscious way of telling the other person we trust them; that we feel safe with them. Shakespeare would say it's because 'Love looks not with the eyes but with the mind.' Some might say it's because love is blind. But I think it's because love is willing to see less and willing to overlook what doesn't matter."

"My father says love is not only blind, it's deaf and dumb."

"My first husband used to say, 'Love is blind until marriage opens your eyes,' Rosa said with a smile. "However, love isn't deaf ... just the opposite. Listening is a synonym for loving. As for love being dumb, your father may be onto something."

Rosa, a *happycondriac,* loved young people and it showed. It didn't bother her when a group of them would hang out around the jukebox, spending more time than money. And although she'd never admitted she had any favorites, she'd taken a real shine to the three musketeers: Graham, T.N., and Grant. Always laughing and teasing one another, she loved watching them together. They had an old shoe comfortability with each other, more like loving brothers than buddies.

Graham had a quiet, introspective streak, with eyes that seldom hinted at what he was thinking. He was able to choose without regret, share freely, and had an infectious laugh that drew people to him. T.N., the obvious scholar of the three, had soft, gentle eyes full of compassion. Of all his good qualities, Rosa was most impressed with his natural ability to listen, really listen to what people told him. Then there was Grant, the curious hellion, always asking questions as he viewed the world as a giant amusement park. Of the three, it was Grant that she worried about the most. She loved the way his mind worked, or rather, the way it didn't work. She was convinced his brain was miss-wired. With hot coals of rebellion in his belly, he not only marched to the beat of a different drummer, but he also did it in his own parade. He challenged everything, especially rules. Often telling him he was the embodiment of misdirection, she'd had difficulty figuring out when he was kidding and when he was serious until she realized he was seldom kidding. What worried her was his borderline contempt for authority, especially the authority that abused people. The only evidence of a temper she'd witnessed was when he'd step from behind his shyness to challenge the unjust or arbitrary.

"Did you tell her you loved her?"

"Not until the next day."

"What did she say?"

"She smiled and said, 'You better.'"

"How does that make you feel?" Rosa asked, knowing he was bursting to tell someone about how wonderful he felt.

Grant shrugged his shoulders. "Kind of like I'm more alive ... but mostly, I think it makes me feel more real," he replied slowly as if he was asking a question instead of answering one.

Rosa nodded her understanding. "They say falling in love turns our lives upside down and, when that happens, we discover that our lives are rooted in love."

Grant did not say anything for several seconds before he asked, "How many times have you fallen in love?"

"I fell a couple of times and a few times, I jumped," Rosa replied, grinning at the boldness of the question. One of Grant's less enduring qualities and he had many, was getting so wrapped up in his private quest to learn more that he'd lose his sensitivity to the feelings of others.

Grant laughed. "Why do they call it falling in love?"

"I guess because it usually isn't something we decide to do. We don't decide to love someone, it just happens and often we feel helpless as it's happening ... like when you're falling."

"How do you know if it's real?"

"They say if you have to ask if you're in love, you're not. I don't know if that's true, but I do know that love will teach you what you need to know about it."

"What about lust? Will it teach me what I need to know about it?" Grant teased.

Rosa smiled again, enjoying how he'd often insert a twist into the conversation. "It will teach you far more than that if you're smart enough to learn its lessons. While love walks hand in hand with lust, lust also walks alone. Learning the difference between them is tricky. The simple answer to your next question," Rosa said, pleased she could read him so well, "is that lust is wanting Cindy, love is wanting what's best for her, and true love is the willingness to let her freely decide what that is. Knowing Cindy as I do, nothing will change her mind about you faster than you trying to curtail that mile-wide streak of independence of hers. If you remember not to take everything, she gives you as if it's yours to take, you'll do fine."

Rosa-isms

Love diminishes another's faults; hate diminishes your virtues

We are shaped by those people and the things we love.

Love isn't blind; it just overlooks. Hate isn't blind either, but all it can see is itself.

If you are willing to lie for a lay, it's lust.

Marriage isn't falling in love forever; it's falling in love over and over again.

Take Me by My Little Hand and Go Like This – Chubby Checker

But only in their dreams can men be truly free. It was always thus and always thus will be.

~Robin Williams (**In** Dead Poets Society)

Born Ernest Evans attended South Philadelphia High School with Frankie Avalon and Fabian. It's reported that Barbara Mallery, Dick Clark's childhood sweetheart and the first of his 3 wives, was the one who suggested to Ernest that he use the stage name Chubby Checker as a takeoff on Fats Domino's name. So Chubby Checker recorded the 1960 chart-topping hit "The Twist."

On Wednesday, February 20, 1963, a sudden snowstorm turned blizzard caught everyone off guard and closed most of the schools in Upstate New York, including Indian River Central High School. However, by the time the elementary students were bussed home, the roads were drifting faster than the snowplows could keep up. Shortly after three that afternoon, Grant's principal informed the student body they were officially "snowed in" until the roads could be reopened. Around nine o'clock that evening, conditions improved enough to allow those students living in one of the four small surrounding towns to be bussed to the center of each town, providing their parents could pick them up. The remaining students living on snow-clogged country roads were "taken in" by people living close to the school, with only a few having to spend the night on mats in the school gym. Grant and two other boys spent the night and much of the next day at the home of one of the school custodians.

The teaching staff, required to stay with the students, sent everyone to the gym for what became a six-hour sock hop. Cindy did her best trying to teach Grant how to do "The Twist," but Grant would never be much of a dancer. Later, the cafeteria staff prepared sandwiches. Grant spent the evening holding hands with Cindy, and, although he didn't know who wrote the book of love, he was sure his and Cindy's picture was in it.

No matter what time it is on the East Coast, it's still the 1960's in my mind.

A Blue, Blue Mood

I don't like it, but I guess things happen that way.

~Johnny Cash

Saturday, May 23, 1964 – Prom Night

Marty Robbins's 1957 hit contained the words that best described Grant at his senior prom in May of 1964. While at the prom with one girl, and wearing the obligatory white sports coat and a pink carnation, Grant was indeed in a blue, blue mood. In his wallet, under the picture of his prom date, was the picture of the girl who had broken up with him months earlier. Wrinkled and tattered, Cindy's picture had survived wallet after wallet of Grant carrying her on his hip since the sixth grade.

Dion and the Belmonts weren't the only ones asking why they had to be a teenager in love. Still popular in 1964, the song not only haunted Grant, it also became his daily mantra. Beyond any power, Grant had to say no, Cindy was Grant's first experiment in opening himself to another. With a lack of intention, she had stumbled into his secret places.

Mrs. MacAllister used poetry to teach her students that love would help them to create meaning in their lives. Rosa told Grant that love would introduce him to his greater self. Henry David Thoreau wrote that "Love must be as much a light as it is a flame." Albert Einstein said, "Gravitation is not responsible for people falling in love." And I Corinthians taught Grant that, "Love is patient; love is kind. It does not envy, it does not boast, it is not proud. It is not rude, it is not self-seeking, it is not easily angered, it keeps no record of wrongs. Love does not delight in evil but rejoices with the truth. It always protects, always trusts, always hopes, always perseveres. Love never fails."

However, not Mrs. MacAllister's poetry, or Rosa's wisdom, or Einstein's insights, or scripture seemed to help Grant all that much as he tried to figure out why something that felt so good could also feel so bad.

After Cindy, suffering from a case of buyer's remorse, broke up with him, Grant understood how Linus felt when his security blanket was in the dryer. Being in love was, for Grant, an emotional roller coaster ride of chaos. One minute he understood what Rosa meant about love introducing him to his greater self and the next he was face-to-face with far more basic desires. Every time Grant put his foot on the gas, Cindy put hers on the break. The only thing stronger than Cindy's will was her won't. To Grant, falling in love often felt like falling apart.

If a girl won't go out with you, you can't stop her.

Temptation can't enter a closed door.

If there's a wolf at your door, my daughter is at home.

To tell the difference between a temptation and an opportunity, count the number of times it knocks.

88% of a man's behavior is designed to get a woman into bed. The remaining 12 % serves no purpose.

Black Stone Saturday Night

> *White was the Roman symbol for happiness; black was the symbol of sadness or misfortune. In a Roman trial, a guilty vote was made with a black stone, a white stone for acquittal. In daily life, "albo lapillo notare diem" meant "to mark a day with a white stone" meaning it was a good day.*

Saturday, March 28, 1964

Grant smiled as Rosa handed him the small, white bag containing a dozen chocolate chip (Toll House) cookies, his favorite. Rosa then pushed his money back across the counter saying, "They're on the house today. Keep this for your college fund."

Knowing it was useless to argue with her, Grant nodded his thanks. Although a modest amount, Grant didn't know that nearly a third of the money he'd saved for college came from Rosa. Grant knew his mother was selling Rosa vegetables from their farm's massive garden in the summer along with eggs and homemade bread year-round, but it would be several years before he'd learn that Rosa was overpaying Maretta as a donation to his college fund. With what his parents gave him, what he earned working for Dr. Pierce, and the money he made doing odd jobs for area farmers, Grant had saved enough to pay for his first year of college.

One or two Saturday evenings a month, Grant would stop at the Chat-A-Wyle for a dozen of Rosa's homemade cookies on his way home from work. For the last eight years, since it debuted on Saturday night television in 1955, it had been a Robinson family tradition to enjoy chocolate ice cream while watching *Gunsmoke*. Although Grant's parents did their week's grocery shopping on

Friday nights, the twenty-five-mile drive home was too far to prevent ice cream from melting. Instead, each Saturday afternoon, a yellow Sealtest Ice Cream truck would pull into their yard, delivering ice cream to Grant's front door for just a dollar per half-gallon. On one side of the truck, it said, "Buy the best ... buy Sealtest" and on the other side, it said, "Smoothest eating this side of heaven."

As far as Grant was concerned, nothing went better with Sealtest chocolate ice cream than a couple of fresh, Original Nestle Toll House Chocolate Chip Cookies. Although there are conflicting versions of how Nestle acquired the recipe printed on each package of its chocolate chips, it's generally agreed that the world owes its thanks to Mrs. Ruth Wakefield who owned and operated the Toll House Inn in Whitman, Massachusetts during the 1930s for giving it the original chocolate chip cookie. In addition to having them for dessert, history indicates that Mrs. Wakefield also gave her customers complimentary cookies to take home with them. Regardless of their origin, Grant was positive that Mrs. Wakefield would be both pleased and proud that Rosa had made her chocolate chip cookies one of two Chat-A-Wyle's signature desserts. The second was Raspberry Pie.

Between its CBS debut on September 10, 1955, and its last show on March 31, 1975, Marshall Matt Dillon kept the peace in Dodge City for 635 episodes of *Gunsmoke*. The cast included James Arness (Matt Dillon), Dennis Weaver (Chester Goode, Matt's deputy), Milburn Stone (Doc Adams), and Amanda Blake (Miss Kitty who owned the Long Branch Saloon). In 1962, during Grant's sophomore year of high school, Festus Haggen (portrayed by Ken Curtis) was introduced to the citizens of Dodge City. Two years later, Festus became a regular cast member and replaced Quint Asper (portrayed by Burt Reynolds) as Grant's favorite *Gunsmoke* character. Another of Grant's favorite *Gunsmoke* characters, the gunsmith Newly O'Brien (portrayed by Buck Taylor) joined the show in 1967. Years later, in 2005, Grant would enjoy visiting with Buck Taylor in Kanab, Utah where they'd reminisced about *Gunsmoke*, the untimely loss of Milburn Stone and Amanda Blake, and about how much they enjoyed being grandfathers. *Gunsmoke* was one of the first of a long string of television westerns. At one point there were thirty westerns on the air at the same time, but none of them compared to *Gunsmoke*, the first adult western. Not only did *Gunsmoke* outlast all the others, when it left the air in 1975 after twenty years, it was also the last remaining Western on television.

As if reading his mind, Rosa nodded toward the bag of cookies. "Go ahead and have one. I gave you a baker's dozen."

All smiles, Grant took the 13th cookie from the bag. "Thanks, Rosa. Next to my mom, nobody makes cookies better than you."

"So, tell me, Mr. Future History Teacher, what's the origin of a baker's dozen?" Rosa teased, knowing that if Grant didn't know the answer, he'd make one up.

After washing down the last of the cookie with cold milk, Grant wiped his mouth with a napkin before replying. "No one knows for sure, but most historians believe the baker's dozen began in 13th century England. Back then, if a baker was caught shortchanging a customer, he could have one of his hands cut off. So, to be on the safe side, bakers began giving their customers a 13th item to assure they didn't accidentally cheat them."

As Rosa listened to Grant's response, she watched his smiling eyes for a glimmer of falsehood but found none.

She had learned to expect Grant to test her, delighting in getting one by her. However, he was not in the mood for his favorite game.

Hiding her awe of Grant's knowledge of historical trivia, Rosa nodded. "That makes sense." Then, changing the subject, Rosa asked, "How come you're not out on a date on a Saturday night?"

Grant's smile faded. "The girl I was supposed to take out tonight isn't speaking to me."

"No wonder you look as somber as a urologist's office. Is she the brunette you were in here with a couple of weeks ago?"

"Yeah; she's from Antwerp."

"In Philippians," she said with a hint of a smile, "we are instructed to 'be thankful unto the Lord for what we have and even more thankful for what we don't have.'"

Grant knew Rosa had not been impressed with his date that night and suspected she was trying to get one by him. When he closed one eye and cocked his head, giving her a doubt-filled look, Rosa laughed saying, "Hey, which one of us used to be the Nun?"

Grant laughed but wasn't convinced she had not made up the Philippian quote.

"So, what is Cindy doing tonight?"

"She's so disinterested in me, she won't even take the time to ignore me," Grant sighed. "I heard she was dating someone else. She and I are no longer me and her."

Trying to win back his smile, Rosa teased, "Smart girl." Then she added, "The course of true love never did run smooth."

Looking up into Rosa's sapphire eyes that took nothing for granted, Grant knew she'd just asked him a question.

Rosa was always asking him questions, always challenging him, always pushing him beyond his comfort level.

"That's from Shakespeare's *A Midsummer Night's Dream*, right?" Grant answered, without being able to hide the uncertainty in his voice.

"Very good, Grant, very good," Rosa chuckled, knowing she had more confidence in his abilities than he did. "But unfortunately, Shakespeare's observation doesn't seem to be giving you any comfort."

"I feel like I did in elementary school when my mother forced me to wear clothes I didn't pick out," Grant said slowly, his voice full of self-pity.

Rosa fought to hold back a smile. "It's pretty obvious you're in pain, jealous of Cindy being with someone else, and that you miss her."

"I guess your friend William would call us "a pair of star-crossed lovers," Grant teased with a weak smile.

Rosa chuckled. "That's the sass I like so much, Romeo, and that would be our friend William. So, have you talked to Juliet lately?"

"The last time I tried, she gave me a look like I'd just kicked one of her cats. Wednesday was her birthday. I sent her a birthday card, but no, we haven't talked in a long time. It looks like she's now the answer to someone else's prayer."

What Grant didn't share was, more than talking with Cindy, he missed how she'd take his hand in silence, rest her head on his shoulder, and just be. Cindy taught Grant how to be comfortable with silence by living in the moment as she willingly joined her solitude with his.

"You could pray to get her back?"

"Maybe I should order a Brother Al Prayer Cloth."

"What's a Brother Al Prayer Cloth?"

"I listened to Brother Al on the radio late one night. He's an evangelist who, if you send him a donation, will send you back five one-inch square prayer cloths. You put them on people without them knowing, like in a pocket of something they are going to wear, and then he prays for them. He claims the power of God is transmitted through the cloths so they will be healed or find a job, or whatever you're praying for."

"Interesting. You buy that?"

"Shakespeare would call it 'an improbable fiction.'"

And the Romans would say, "*Amantes sunt amentes*," Rosa countered.

Grant, who had dropped the second year of Latin to take Mrs. MacAllister's class on "The Works of Shakespeare," said, "Amantes is lovers and *sunt* is are, but I don't know the word *amentes*."

"It means 'lunatics,' meaning you can't be in love and wise at the same time."

"Then perhaps I should pray for wisdom."

"There are more things in heaven and earth, Horatio," Rosa said as she patted the back of his hand.

Rosa-isms

Our greatest regrets are often the offspring of our deepest desires.

Grant, your sour grapes have given you a bumper crop of the whines.

Charm may get you the girl, but it isn't enough to keep her.

Unattended fires go out.

Shaken, Not Stirred

> *Life is serious, but that doesn't prevent it from also being funnier than hell. Without a sense of humor, you're what Julius Caesar would call raptus regaliter (royally screwed).*

The turn of events leading to April 11, 1964, began several months earlier with an answer to a casual question at one of John Kennedy's Press Conferences. Kennedy, when asked what he liked to read, replied he enjoyed Ian Fleming's books about James Bond. Grant, who loved all things Kennedy, was delighted when Meredith, his best friend because neither felt a need to prove anything to the other and who owned the keenest wit and most untraditionally ordered mind Grant had ever encountered, announced that he had several Bond books Grant could borrow. They were like potato chips to Grant; he couldn't read just one as he began consuming a James Bond paperback a week.

The top five songs that year were, "Under the Boardwalk" (The Drifters), "Chapel of Love" (The Dixie Cups), "Leader of the Pack" (The Shangri-las), "Bread and Butter" (The Newbeats), and "Little Old Lady from Pasadena" (Jan and Dean). Also in 1964, "do-wah diddy-diddy dum diddy-do" echoed across the country, *Jeopardy* debuted, the first Ford Mustang rolled off the assembly line, the Monokini (topless bathing suit) was introduced, Bob Dylan introduced *marijuana* to the Beatles, and the *Warren Commission Report* was published finding that Lee Harvey Oswald acted alone in assassinating President Kennedy.

As he began devouring Fleming's books, Grant was also knee-deep into Bob Dylan. In Grant's mind, James Bond and Bob Dylan became one as they nourished the growing rebellion within his soul. He wasn't alone; soon an entire generation would be quoting James Bond and singing along with Dylan. However, in the backwaters of Northern New York, both Bond and Dylan were still relatively unknown. Except for his best friend, Meredith, Grant didn't know anyone who knew what the two zeros in 007 meant. Nor, with the exception of Cindy, did he know anyone who listened to Dylan's music.

The top movies in 1964 were *My Fair Lady, Zorba the Greek, The Pink Panther, Becket,* and *Dr. Stranglove.* That year also saw the introduction of Zip codes, Lucky Charms, the Kennedy half dollar, go-go girls, and Pop-Tarts. The new *Gilligan's Island* was a smash hit and *The Dick Van Dyke Show* took top honors for the best comedy. Other top comedy shows included *The Munsters, Petticoat Junction,* and *My Three Sons,* the Beatles appeared on the *Ed Sullivan Show,* the Rolling Stones released their first album, Cassius Clay defeated Sonny Liston to become the heavyweight champion of the world, and the plans for building the World Trade Center were made public.

What began as a snowstorm had quickly turned to rain by midmorning. Although an April snowstorm wasn't unusual in the "lake effect" areas of Northern New York, this one had left as fast as it had come. By early evening, the roads were wet but free of snow and ice. The rain slowed to a stop by five o'clock and what little sunlight there was soon lost to deepening darkness and dropping temperatures. It would be years before Grant would first hear the term black ice and then he thought it was the name of a new rock group. Three days earlier, the second Bond movie, *From Russia with Love,* was released in American theaters. Meredith, Grant, and their dates left the movie in Gouverneur around 9:30 that evening. The guys were far more impressed with the movie than were their dates, mostly because they had read the book. They hadn't gone far nor was Meredith driving too fast for the conditions when they had an up-close and personal experience with black ice.

In 1964, baby boomers were doing the Dog, the Monkey, the Frug, and the Watusi and singing along to "I Get Around", "Downtown", "I Want To Hold Your Hand", and "King of the Road." That year, the Supreme Court upheld the Civil Rights Act, the United States began bombing North Vietnam, Martin Luther King Jr. became the youngest recipient of the Nobel Peace Prize, and Meredith was a marksman in training for the Olympics Trials. Earlier that day, Grant had gone with him to a four-hour practice at a local firing range. When they returned home, Meredith inadvertently left his rifle in the backseat. Later, when picking up their dates, Grant placed the rifle on the back window ledge.

It was one of those "all of a sudden," slow motions accidents. The road was bare, except for a small stretch of black ice lying in wait for an unsuspecting driver. At the beginning of a long, lazy turn, Meredith was unable to do anything except grip the steering wheel and watch with his passengers as the car slowly slid off the road and crashed through the bottom of a large, wooden billboard advertising Pall Mall Cigarettes.

The damage to the sign was minor, limited to the wooden lattes under it. The car suffered some dents and scratches on the right fender and the right headlight had to be replaced. However, the damage inside the car was far more extensive. When the car finally came to a stop, both Grant, his date, and the rifle were thrown toward the front seat. Although the rifle was in a leather case, when it hit Grant in the back, it took out two of Grant's discs at L4 and

L5. The next morning Grant was admitted to the hospital where he spent the next fifteen days in traction, the first of several such hospital stays Grant would have over the next five years.

You never stop paying your dues because life never stops sending you renewal notices.

If all the cried-over spilled milk were collected each year, it would make enough cottage cheese to fill the Roman Coliseum nine times.

Yo-Yo

There's a difference between loving others for all you're worth and loving others for all they're worth.

~Ray Duncan

Yo-yo's lifelong love of driving fast has been transferred to the plane he flies as co-owner of a small crop-dusting business in St. Lawrence County. However, the majority of his business is flying tourists over the Thousand Islands and flying over parades, sporting events, and other large gatherings dragging large banners ranging from "I love you, Sylvia, will you marry me?" to "Buy Local: Shop at Whatchamajiggers' Hardware." The last time T.N. rode with him, Yo-yo had burned his own CDs of Golden Oldies. They were divided into the four categories; School Zone, Fast, Bat out of Hell, and Good Morning Judge, one for each of his four driving speeds.

Today JD is a retired Methodist minister who, in addition to an occasional wedding or funeral, supplements his pension as a disc jockey for area parties and dances. The Yellow Pages ad and the red magnetic signs on the sides of his pickup read, "For the Best Sounds Around, call JD the DJ." Known for being an outstanding pastor, part of JD's success came from very few of his parishioners knowing more about sin than him.

Yo-yo is now a retired entomologist of some renown in the bug world. He first discovered his interest in insects while fighting to survive as a prisoner of war in Vietnam. Against all odds and in keeping with the meaning of his Tagalog nickname, Yo-yo managed to come back. Yo-yo recently celebrated his twenty-fourth wedding anniversary. Of which Ray said, "Not bad for a turn the other cheek Lutheran and an eye-for-an-eye Baptist." At fifty-nine, it's his first and Harley's second marriage. High school sweethearts until the death of Harley's mother led them in different directions; Harley left Benign to spend her days raising clouds of dust while Yo-yo spent his raising hell.

Harley and Yo-yo re-ignited the embers that Yo-yo had nourished since high school when they reunited at their ten-year class reunion. During the years following his return from Vietnam, Yo-yo had been good at looking for a wife and bad at finding one. In and out of several relationships, he'd never been able to close the deal because, as he said at his wedding, "Shackled by yesterday, I kept a room ready in my heart for ten years, waiting for Harley to move back in." Then, with a wide smile, he added, "Like me, she came back."

The Duncan brothers haven't always lived "good," but they've lived well. Both are still bright, friendly, and easygoing. As a minister and an entomologist, one has gone through life looking up, the other looking down. Still each other's best friend, one puts others first and the other puts himself last.

Yo-yo-isms

Wishing blows out candles while expectations light them.

If you want to be found, go where people are looking.

Happiness is pre-mediated.

Wednesday, July 18, 2007 – Lost in The Fifties Tonight

Scares are tattoos of the lessons I've learned.

~Karen Mal

Harley no longer meets each morning as if it were an icy cold wind. Harley no longer spends lonely nights listening to heat pipes cough or neon signs buzzing like giant insects in cheap hotel rooms off the interstate. Harley no longer lives in the shadow of what was or what might have been as memories of Buffalo, Chicago, Tampa, Tulsa, Winslow, Toronto, Boston, Charleston, St. Louis, Louisville, Nashville, Reno, Fargo, Dodge City, Sioux City, Sarasota, Santa Fe, and a hundred other cities fade to black.

Ray Duncan (Yo-yo) no longer lives with an empty, reckless feeling of something missing in his life. Ray's home no longer feels like a concrete bunker where he seeks to shape-shift into someone else. Ray no longer spends his days walking a thin line between solitude and loneliness. Ray no longer hovers between the seasons, his heart pretending to beat, as he gazes at the horizon like a junkie searching for a vein.

Harley was conceived on a back road in the backseat of the same Ford her father was driving away in the last time her mother saw him. He left on a far chillier afternoon than expected for such a sunny day. There were still slivers of snow in the shade-sheltered places, evidence that winter wasn't surrendering easily to the invading spring. Harley's mother didn't surrender easily either. She attended college as a single mother and graduated with the single dream of being a schoolteacher. Her dream was realized, her mother made a life for herself and Harley. However, fate soon began having its way with Harley's mother. Forced to leave teaching because of advancing cancer, Harley's mother left chalk dust, morning announcements, and the smell of Elmer's Glue behind when she left life at the age of thirty-five. She also left behind an eighteen-year-old Harley to find her way on her own.

Born on April 7, 1942, Harley learned quickly how to open doors with a wink and a smile. She also learned to fight better than anyone she couldn't outrun and to outrun anyone better than her in a fight. But like her misspent youth, Harley has left fighting and running behind. She now approaches a problem as her old blue tick hound lays down. She skirts its perimeter, circling and sniffing it before easing into seeking a solution. Harley now greets each new day with a full heart, a warm smile, and a strength of character forged in the fire of the hell she survived.

John Kennedy was President for two years, ten months, and two days. Harley had lived each of those days plus seven more waiting with unspoiled hope. She'd met Todd in a pancake house in Oklahoma City on August 18, 1961, immediately fell in love with him, married him a year later on the eve of his deployment to Vietnam, and lost him when an Army Chaplin handed her a yellow telegram on November 27, 1963. Serving as one of three hundred military advisors Kennedy had sent to Vietnam, Todd died in a helicopter crash. Harley's grief was more than she could fight so she tried outrunning it. She took little with her as she took to the open road on Todd's motorcycle. For the next five years, Harley's life seemed like one long yesterday since she'd kissed Todd goodbye. Although Harley's memories of her first marriage only sporadically tease her into opening them, on the top shelf of her closet there's a small tin-box museum of old photographs and tattered letters she no longer visits.

Harley wasn't a virgin when she met Todd. She and Ray, high school sweethearts, had exchanged virginities in the backseat of Ray's car the night of their senior prom. They had pledged their undying love, believing they would one day marry. However, following her mother's death, Harley moved to Oklahoma City to live with her aunt. As the days turned to weeks and then to months, Harley sent Ray fewer and fewer letters until she became his favorite memory and he became her first used to be.

Harley's two passions, following Todd's death, were his 1960 steel and chrome Indian motorcycle and her music. Looking like a blue-eyed Madonna with her Harlow-gold hair tucked up under a red, white, and blue bandana, Harley was on intimate terms with the night as she carried her pain around inside the words she could not bring herself to speak. Full of lost dreams and forgotten pleasures, Harley lived in exile; homeless and wandering in search of some imagined promised land. When Jefferson said, "a little rebellion now and then is a good thing" he was talking about politics. However, his words were also true of Harley. When Thomas Paine wrote, "We have it within our power to begin the world all over again," he was talking about people like Harley.

Although she couldn't speak her pain, she could sing it. Besides her memories, her constant companions were an old six-string, a raspy voice reminiscent of Kim Carnes and Janis Joplin, and her songs. As she made her way back and forth across the country, Harley's life became an unending series of coffee houses, darkened bars, smoky taverns, folk festivals, and county fairs where she sang about our fears, our differences, and the sameness of our tears. She sang about our common threads, histories, and mysteries, about our futures and our yesterdays, about human rights, birthrights, and the weary, wounded warrior within each of us. Using her stage name, Harley sang about loves lost and found, victories and defeats, and about the hungry, the haunted, and the broken-hearted.

Whether Harley outran her grief, or it grew tired of chasing her, she now possesses the air of someone who belongs wherever she goes. Harley has what F. Scott Fitzgerald calls, "a willingness of the heart." Joyfully remarried with three children and two grandchildren, Harley now lives in the present, loving the world one day at a time. From the Vietnam Conflict to our second invasion of Iraq, Harley has marched, sung, and protested against war after war. She speaks out for Todd and all those forever silenced, she sings for Todd and all those forever still, and she cries for Todd and all those sent in our country's name to kill and die. Every time Harley lights a candle she's reminded of Ray and later, when she blows it out, she's reminded of Todd.

It wasn't a lack of suitors that prevented Harley from entering another relationship. Except for her music, Harley had lost her will to love. Once an ordinary girl with ordinary dreams, Harley felt she was past the point of no return as life's consequences, like the ocean, rolled over her in waves, one behind the other. However, state-by-state, town-by-town, and song-by-song Harley began coming to terms with her grief until she was able to put her life in perspective.

One morning somewhere on the desert near Tonopah, Arizona, Harley, with a yearning undefined, turned eastward into the rising sun. A week later, she road into Benign and back into Ray's life as the girl from yesterday. Although she hadn't returned in search of Ray, she soon realized she was in search of the idea of Ray. After five years of living by her wits and a six-string, Harley returned to Benign on one of those early spring mornings that arrive wearing a t-shirt and shorts. No one knows what it was about her hometown that spoke to Harley, but it was here that she decided to unfurl her days in search of a new life.

Harley spent her first six nights camping in Veterans Park next to the river before cramming her dreams into a small apartment over the Benign Post Office. She then took a job at Butterfield's Drug Store where she again discovered Ray Duncan. A few months later, they went on a tentative date to their ten-year class reunion. It was less of a date than it was a prearranged accidental meeting.

Ray Duncan never mastered the art of beginning anything at the beginning. Nor, with a glint of madness in his eyes, did he go anywhere with a sense of purpose. But that ended as Harley taught him to ride a motorcycle and he taught her how to fly, both having realized they were each other's last plane out. For the first time in years, another person became Harley's epicenter. For the first time in years, Ray began making decisions without consulting his constant companions, Eeny, Meeny, Miney, and Moe. And, for the first time in years, they both knew the difference between living and serving time.

After losing Harley, Ray had worked at odd jobs until he was drafted into the army at the height of the Vietnam Conflict. Listed as Missing in Action, it would be four long years before Ray would find his way home again. Ray had grown into manhood as a POW in a foreign land while Harley had grown into womanhood feeling like a foreigner in her own land. While in college, good grades came easier for Ray than making the grade with any of the women he dated. Harley, his first kiss, had set the bar higher than any other woman could attain, so, after a short romance, Ray would live out the same old played-out scenes as he moved on to another.

"Sometimes the world gets crazy, but then so do I," Harley was singing with a smile when Ray walked into the VFW hall where she was making her hometown début. While drinking beer from a Styrofoam cup, Ray listened to a long-lost voice soaking into his broken places. Years later, on the eve of her daughter's wedding, Harley was asked why she'd agreed to date Ray again. Without hesitation, she replied, "When I was lost, he never stopped looking for me."

Harley-isms

What you're seeking is what's driving you to look.

Love is more complicated than an Arabian fairytale.

You don't understand how to touch until you've felt what isn't there.

You can't be a better person and a bitter one at the same time.

Don't chase two rabbits at the same time.

CHAPTER SIX

Not In My Name

Benign Was More Than a Town; It Was a Time.

Benign was more than a town, it was a time when we took pride in the knowledge our country wouldn't start a war by invading another country or force its way of life on other peoples. It was a time when we loved our country, not out of fear, but out of the belief that it made it possible for everyone to turn the American dream into a reality. It was a time when opposing injustice and standing alone with right on your side was the only majority one needed. It was a time when children were not allowed to sit on their duffs, go gallivanting around the neighborhood, or go gadding about as free as a bird.

Benign was a time when stompers were shoes, threads were clothes, anything outdated was old hat, smooth meant good, being in the groove meant you were doing well, suspenders were pulleys, hoofing meant walking, and to hoof meant to dance. It was a time when gobbledygook was anything not making sense, grandstanding was showing off, an old-fashioned person was a fuddy-duddy, corny was silly, and if you "Ameched." someone, you called them on the phone. (Don Ameche played Bell in the movie, *The Story of Alexander Grant Bell* in 1939.)

Benign was a time of Disney's Davy Crockett, *Texaco Star Theater*, polio shots given in schools, S&H Green Stamps, *Peyton Place*, Dick Clark's *American Bandstand*, Swanson TV dinners, Perry Como's *The Kraft Music Hall*, cowcatchers on trains, pneumatic tubes running along the walls and ceilings of department stores, *Bazooka Joe* comic strips inside individually-wrapped pieces of Bazooka bubblegum, and Cool Hand Luke's, "What we've got here is a failure to communicate."

Benign was a time of Tuesday nights with Red Skelton, who closed each program with "Good night and may God bless," after entertaining the country with such characters as Clem Kadiddlehopper, Willy Lump-Lump, Sheriff Deadeye, Cauliflower McPugg, and San Fernando Red. It was also a time when a young writer for Red Skelton named Johnny Carson was making his mark.

Saturday, March 25, 2006 - The Second Chance

Grant and T.N. were enjoying their lunch at The Second Chance.

"Although I agree that Dylan is most likely the jester, how does the king's thorny crown being stolen, and the courtroom be adjourned without a verdict fit with Kennedy being the king?"

After taking a long sip of his cream soda, T.N. replied, "Both Kennedy and Dylan were extremely popular with young people. Perhaps McLean was saying that Dylan's voice had replaced Kennedy's with our generation, meaning he had stolen Kennedy's crown. However, the lyrics also give credence to those who believe that Lee Harvey Oswald was the jester. By killing him, Oswald had stolen Kennedy's crown. In addition, the courtroom being adjourned before a verdict was returned, is a good description of Oswald being killed before he could stand trial. For those believing, like you, that Dylan was the jester, McLean could have been referring to Dylan wanting to be more famous than Elvis, thus stealing his crown."

"Both theories make sense," Grant agreed while wondering why he had never put either meaning to McLean's lyrics. "So, who's the quartet in the park?"

"Many believe it's the Beetles."

Grant asked, "Does helter-skelter refer to a Beatles song, or does it have something to do with Charles Manson?"

"Perhaps both," T.N. replied. "Helter Skelter was on the Beatles' 1968 'White Album.' Manson claimed the Devil talked to him through that song, which led him and his followers to kill Sharon Tate and four others. The 'summer swelter' probably refers to the 'Summer of Love' or the movie, *Long Hot Summer*."

"I understand that, but what's the fallout shelter?"

"I'm not sure, other than being some reference to the fascination our parents had for fallout shelters in the 50s. But the birds being eight miles up and then falling fast likely refers to the Byrds and their song, 'Eight Miles High.'"

"And the players trying for a forward pass?"

"Many think it's a metaphor for the Rolling Stones trying to replace the Beatles. That seems a little farfetched to me. Instead of being about the Beatles, I think it's about Dylan."

"How so?"

"There were a lot of folk singers who had a hard time making it big because they couldn't compete with Dylan. And, with Dylan incapacitated for several months following a serious motorcycle accident in 1966, they finally got the chance they needed."

Grant chuckled. "And thus the line, 'With the jester on the sidelines in a cast.'"

"Bingo!"

"Bingo? That's what Rosa used to say."

T.N. smiled. "Yeah, she sure did. If you get a chance, you should visit her before you leave. She'd love that you remember her. She's on the left, just past the Bodine plot near the upper entrance. Look for the headstone with the word, 'Bingo' on it."

Grant laughed out loud. "She had a great sense of humor. Rosa could slice a piece of cake in such a way that everyone believed they'd received the biggest piece. I miss her for a lot of reasons, but mostly for the impact she had on my life."

My addiction to diners like this one began right here with Rosa. There's a diner in Tucson I frequent far too often, but I can't help myself. In addition to the waitresses, the food, and the music, I love watching people enter and exit like the tides. Within any three days, you'll find college students studying for an exam in one of the large corner booths, desert doves and their pimps, ex-husbands who don't want to cook on their day with the kids, snowbirds seeking refuge from northern winters, and the homeless seeking a few minutes of shelter from the harsh Tucson sun over a free cold glass of water. There are low-level managers in cheap suits, swaggering young men with more moo than milk, riders from the bus depot next door, back-booth prophets, coffee only book readers, gun rack pickup truckers, hardhats, counter-stool philosophers, laptopers, the hopelessly unemployed, the in-between jobbers, salespeople from the mall across the street, and curious idlers like myself."

Thirsty Shoes

And the day came when the risk it took to remain tight inside the bud was more painful than the risk it to blossom.

~Anais Nin

October 7, 1960

It was a night of firsts that would last Grant a lifetime. It was the night he first decided he'd someday drive the entire length of Route 66, the night he became a Democrat, the first time he watched a televised presidential debate, and the first (and hopefully last) time he'd have his eyebrows burned off. It was a night of pain, exploration, rebirth, and wonder. Now, over fifty years later, Grant can still remember Quemoy, Matsu, the smell of burning hair, and his first glimpse of Holbrook, Arizona.

Each life journey is filled with moments that seep into our souls, changing our direction and helping us to focus upon new horizons. Although these moments are uniquely our own, there are also those moments that are so monumental that they can imprint an entire generation. For Grant's grandparents, the Market Crash of 1929 and the death of FDR were such moments. For Grant's parents, Pearl Harbor was a monumental moment destined to reshape their view of the world. For Grant's generation, the moment occurred when an assassin snuffed out the life of John Kennedy. Another moment came a decade later as they watched Neil Armstrong take a giant leap for mankind. And for the next generation, their moment came via classroom televisions as the image of the Challenger Disaster destroyed their trust in science.

Grant's parents had been shopping at the Bradley Street Department Store where they'd purchased a roll of linoleum for their kitchen floor. While helping their dad unroll it, Grant and Dennis were more interested in fooling around than in helping out. Deciding he'd be better off without them, Stanley told them to burn the papers, including the twelve-foot cardboard box that had contained the linoleum. After watching the box burn in their burning barrel for a few minutes, Grant took his first steps down a path he still follows. Having only burned on one end, it was still eight or nine feet long when Grant pulled the box from the flames. Now dark, he lit up their front yard when he threw it upward into the night. While soaring, the open end ate enough oxygen to make it glow bright red. Then, halfway between going up and coming down, it hung in the sky, suspended for just a moment before surrendering to forces it could neither resist nor understand.

A few minutes before Stanley would mutter, "Idiots! I'm raising idiots!" Grant and Dennis decided to spice up their game by throwing the blazing tube back and forth between them, trying to catch it without getting burned. The trick was to let the burning end pass overhead before jumping upward to grasp the ever-shrinking backend of the box. Grant found this to be great sport until he misjudged the distance and, instead of catching the safe end, the flaming end caught him in the face. Grant can still vividly remember the smell of burning flesh and his last view of the fiery ball just before it singed his hair, burned off most of his eyebrows, and melted away a large area of skin on his forehead. Installation of the new linoleum immediately came to a halt as Maretta applied ice packs to the evidence of the stupidity Stanley was yelling about.

For the next couple of hours, between ice pack treatments and lectures, Grant was exiled to the couch in front of the television. As he winced in pain while watching *Route 66*, his favorite television program, Grant decided he'd someday see the United States and get his "kicks on Route 66." Grant fell in love with the idea of going west on Route 66. He especially wanted to see the Petrified Forest near Holbrook, Arizona, the backdrop of that night's *Route 66* episode.

Following the broadcast of *Route 66*, Channel 7 televised the second Kennedy-Nixon Debate. Grant wouldn't have watched it had he had other options. While growing up in their part of Northern New York, the only two channels the Robinsons received were Channel 7, a CBS station out of Watertown, and Channel 11, a Canadian station out of Kingston, Ontario. Until that debate, Grant, like the rest of his family, favored Nixon. But as he watched them argue over whether the United States should protect Quemoy and Matsu, two islands off the coast of China, Grant and millions of other Americans discovered Kennedy. At that moment Grant hung suspended in time, halfway between what he believed and what he felt, before surrendering to forces he couldn't resist or understand. That night, Grant started his life as a born-again Democrat.

Over the coming months, Grant began challenging his parents' political beliefs, only to later discover that many more such challenges lay ahead. Grant's family didn't believe in conversions, challenges, or Catholic Presidents. Although he didn't know it then, his first steps into the Democratic Party were also his first steps out of the family. To this day Grant's father blames Democrats for women's lib, the decline of America's morals, AIDS, greedy labor unions, free love, losing the war in Vietnam, the Civil Rights Movement, wasteful government spending, high taxes, women at West Point, poor roads, rising divorce rates, and the high cost of lumber.

Grant's desire to leave Northern New York and travel, west across the country, led his grandmother to begin calling him Thirsty Shoes. If his grandmother was looking down on him today, she was also smiling as Grant enjoyed that thirst-quenching moment of driving into Holbrook, Arizona on Route 66.

Stanley-isms

A company without a union is like an ass without a pain.

Alimony is like selling the cow to make payments on a milking machine.

Liberal politics make astrology look good.

Television programs reflect our morals while commercials reflect our values.

You Are What Eats At You

prejudice, n. you don't have it, it has you.

If he had a name, Grant didn't know it. All Grant ever heard him called was nigger. That's all Grant ever called him. It was more a title than a name. Being one of two "coloreds" in Benign, "The Nigger" was the only name needed for everyone to know whom you were talking about. He was only half nigger. His mother was white and his father was long gone. They lived on the outskirts of acceptability, about a mile from town. In the 50s, being part white meant you were all bad, even in Benign.

He was a tenth grader and had missed his bus. He'd waited for the elementary run to catch a ride to the corner of his road, as close to his house as the bus ever went. He was looking at the spot next to Grant with a hope-filled expression as he came down the aisle. Grant was new to the sixth grade, new to riding a school bus and knew better than to let The Nigger sit with him. Grant turned sideways, putting his legs across the seat hoping he wouldn't sit down. He didn't. As he slid into the seat across the aisle from Grant, he smiled. Grant didn't return the smile, nor did he respond to The Nigger's repeated efforts at making friendly conversation. Although he was big, Grant was less afraid of him than of what the other kids would say if he even pretended to be friendly. Grant had seen others make that mistake, only to be rewarded with chants of "Nigger Lover," with Grant a part of the chorus.

Early the next morning Mr. Fields went from room to room, quietly announcing that the "colored" boy from the high school had committed suicide the night before. He asked the kids to bow their heads in silent prayer. They did.

God was alive and well in the schools in those days. That day, Grant suspected that most of them were praying no more niggers would come to their school.

The suicide was a big story in the local newspapers and on television. No one could remember there ever having been a suicide in Benign before. Everyone was sad, made sadder Grant thought, by the suicide note. The Nigger had gotten off their bus that night, written his mother a note, and then hung himself in his room. His note said he couldn't take it anymore. He said he was tired of being teased, tormented, and called a nigger. He also said he didn't have a single friend and that no one, unless they were ridiculing him, would speak to him. After the funeral, they stopped calling him The Nigger, but if he had a name, they didn't know it. They just called him the poor colored boy.

"Before you leave town, you should go walk around the old school," T.N. suggested after they'd shared breakfast at The Second Chance.

"Great idea; it's been so long, I probably won't recognize it."

"They've made some changes over the years, including a six-room addition on the northwest corner, where the old, outdoor wooden bleachers used to be. And the old band room that was over the kitchen is gone, but other than that, it looks pretty much the same."

Three days later, Grant walked to the old school over sidewalks that hadn't been repaired in years. Most were time-cracked, and many had been broken and lifted by large, twisted tree roots. Looking across the playground, the names of classmates he couldn't remember were replaced by the smiling faces he couldn't forget. The school was closed for the summer, but the custodian let Grant inside to wander around in his memories. T.N. had been right; it looked pretty much the same.

Grant sat for a while in his old sixth-grade room. It was in that room that he'd decided he'd someday become a teacher. It was in that room that he'd fallen in love for the first time. And it was in that room that he'd prayed for a boy he'd helped kill. Grant knew they'd all helped, but only Grant knew he'd been the last one to refuse to talk to him. Grant would spend his life wondering if the kid known as The Nigger would have killed himself if Grant would only have had the courage to be friendly to him. Before leaving, Grant wrote, *"If we believe absurdities we shall commit atrocities. – Voltaire"* on the blackboard in remembrance of a nameless black boy. Under it, he wrote, *"NEVER AGAIN – Grant"* in large letters.

It didn't happen overnight, but it began that night as Grant read about the suicide note in the paper. It began as a whisper, a small voice repeating, "Never Again." That black boy's death and Grant's part in it not only changed Grant's life, it, in large part, also defined it. Although only a sixth-grader, that night Grant promised himself he'd never again walk in fear. Never again, would he allow others, including family and friends, to do his thinking. Never again would he be controlled by popular opinion. Never again would he be afraid of what others might say. Never again, would he be afraid to challenge, and if necessary, defy authority. Never again would he allow hatred and bigotry to rule his behavior or place limitations upon what he believed to be right. In the years to come, Grant wouldn't always be successful at hearing or following its urgings, but that voice would always be there, among the chorus, never still, forever whispering, "Never Again."

Rosa-isms

That which sounds hateful to you, speak not to another.

That which is painful to you, do not do to another.

That which diminishes you do not diminish in another.

That which angers you, do not use against another.

That which saddens you, do not visit upon another.

Friday, August 28, 1963 - Not in My Name

A time comes when silence is betrayal, and that time has come for us in relation to Vietnam.

~Martin Luther King, Jr.

Just a short sixty-three days before an assassin would snuff out the life of Robert Kennedy, another assassin, James Earl Ray, would kill Martin Luther King Jr. as he stood on the balcony of the Lorraine Motel in Memphis, Tennessee. Although his murder came as no surprise, it was ironic that a man who preached nonviolence as the primary tactic of the Civil Rights movement would die such a violent death.

In 1965, King, as a matter of conscience and over the objections of many in the civil rights movement, began questioning America's involvement in Vietnam. Afraid that he might compromise their fight for equality, several black leaders cautioned King against coming out against the war. Nevertheless, exactly one year to the day before his death, King made a speech at Riverside Church in New York City entitled "Beyond Vietnam: A Time to Break Silence". Perhaps one of his least known speeches, it was nevertheless a very important speech and a tipping point moment for Grant. A junior in college, Grant had already added his voice to the rapidly growing number of his generation who were speaking out against the war in Vietnam.

Although King's speech received a great deal of attention on the evening news for a few days, other events soon pushed it off the national radar. That same month, Soviet cosmonaut Vladimir Komarov was killed when his Soyuz 1 spacecraft crashed after its parachute failed to deploy on reentry, Muhammad Ali refused induction into the armed forces for religious reasons, and Groucho Marx was the mystery guest on *What's My Line*? Two weeks after his "Beyond Vietnam" speech, King led thousands as they marched to the United Nations building in New York City in protest of the war and the 436 casualties in Vietnam that month.

A week before the first day of his senior year, while Stanley was at work, the rest of Grant's family went to Watertown to take advantage of the department stores' back-to-school sales. He and his mother had argued about Grant staying home, one of a growing number of arguments Grant was having with his parents since he announced his conversion to being a Democrat. Grant wanted to stay home to watch as what Martin Luther King Jr. said would, "go down in history as the greatest demonstration for freedom in the history of our nation." Grant tried, without success, to convince his mother that history would be made that day and he wanted to watch it happen. As she headed for the car with his brother and two sisters, she angrily told him, "Have it your way, but don't whine to me when school starts and you don't have anything to wear."

King had been right. An estimated quarter of a million people from all over the country marched from the Washington Monument to the Lincoln Memorial that day, in yet another milestone in the fight for equality by black Americans.

Grant was having his usual Chat-A-Wyle Cheeseburger, fries, and cream soda the next evening when he was joined by Crackers. The two of them decided to have a quick dinner before picking up their dates for a late Saturday night movie.

As Rosa approached them with menus, she heard them engaged in light-hearted banter.

"I see you two are at it again. Haven't you got anything better to do on a Saturday night? Why don't you have hot dates?" Rosa asked.

Crackers laughed. "We have dates, don't know how hot yet."

Rosa smiled. "Just don't make it too hot. Don't do anything with your dates that you wouldn't want some guy doing with your sister."

"Ouch, talk about throwing cold water on someone," Grant chuckled.

"I'm glad I don't have a sister," Crackers replied.

"Just mind your P's and Q's mister."

"Don't worry, he will," Grant grinned. "If he doesn't, Lisa's father will kill him."

"Yeah, if her mother doesn't beat him to it," Crackers added with a smile.

"There's a difference between doing what's right and being afraid of doing what's wrong," Rosa told him as she looked over at the two men entering the side entrance off of the parking lot reserved for long haulers.

Crackers followed her gaze and then watched the two truckers take a seat in a corner booth. Seeing their eighteen-wheeler, its motor still running, parked outside, he murmured, "I've got to hand it to those guys; driving one of those rigs has got to be a hard life."

"It's nothing I'm interested in doing," Grant said dismissively without looking over at the men.

After taking their order, Rosa poured each of the truckers a cup of free coffee before she gave Marty, the cook, the order slip. Rosa's husband also drove an eighteen-wheeler for a living so she had a soft spot for his fellow truckers, which explained the free coffee. Smiling at Crackers and Grant, she asked, "Did either of you watch the March yesterday?"

"I did. King gave an amazing speech," Grant replied.

"I didn't. I doubt anything he said will make much of a difference in the long run."

"I don't know if King's policy of civil disobedience will make a difference in the life of our country, but I do know it will make a difference in the lives of those who practice it," Rosa replied.

"How so?" asked Crackers.

"Because doing the right thing, especially if it's difficult, builds integrity and integrity is the cornerstone of character."

"I don't think I could face the beatings, the dogs, or water hoses without hitting back," Grant admitted. "I get so pissed off ... uh, angry," Grant corrected just in time to prevent a lecture from Rosa on appropriate vocabulary. "I watch the demonstrations on television and I get so mad I want to burn something down."

"I understand how you feel, but "Deuteronomy" teaches us, 'burning only begets burning.' But at least you're moved to want to do something. Being pissed off is at least a recognition of the injustice," Rosa said straight-faced as she picked up a pot of fresh coffee and left them to walk around the diner, giving out free refills.

As soon as she was far enough away, both boys laughed at Rosa swearing. Hearing her swear was a first for both of them. They were also laughing at her Bible reference. Although Rosa was an ex-nun and knew her *Bible* backward and forward, they knew she was joking. She'd often make up scripture to illustrate a point. When she returned, she found Grant and Crackers arguing over the timing of King's March.

"They'd be better off working to change the laws instead

of tying up traffic in Washington making speeches," Crackers argued.

Rosa listened to them as she wiped the counter clean before refilling their glasses, a Coke for Crackers and a Cream Soda for Grant. Looking at Crackers, she said, "Doing the right thing is often a matter of timing. Think about that tonight on your date. It's easier to do the right thing in the light of day because temptations are always stronger in the dark."

Crackers didn't know how to respond, so he decided to say nothing.

After a few seconds of silence, giving Crackers time to find the real point buried in what she'd said, Rosa continued. "We don't have to go to every fight we're invited to, but sometimes the fight is so important that we cannot walk away from it. Civil Rights is one of those."

"How do you know which fights to fight and when to walk away?"

"It's as easy or as difficult as deciding what's right and what's wrong. When you believe something is wrong, you stand against it any way you can."

"What if you don't know if it's right or wrong?" Grant asked.

"My father says learning to do the right thing takes practice … or something like that," Crackers added.

"I think he is right because, after a while, you'll learn that you are no longer choosing between right and wrong, but between wrong and freedom. At that point, choosing right over what's popular is always a path worth taking, even if it means that sometimes your walk will be lonely. Standing by others requires you first to be willing to stand by yourself. Next year in college, no doubt in Psychology 101, you'll be exposed to the writings of Erich Fromm who wrote, 'Human history begins with man's act of disobedience which is at the very same time the beginning of his freedom and development of his reason.'" Then, with a big smile, she added, "Or something like that."

Grant and Crackers glanced at each other, both once again impressed with Rosa's ability to dish out quotes as easily as she dished out her potato salad. Both of them had, on occasion, wondered if Rosa was as smart as it seemed or if she was good at making up quotes, like she did scripture, to fit whatever position she was taking at the time.

If Rosa noticed their amazement, she didn't acknowledge it as she continued with, "After a while, when you're addicted to the sweet taste of freedom, doing what's right will come naturally. That also includes challenging a wrong, even when your actions won't change or prevent it. The universe, or in my case God, only requires us to do the best we can against injustice, not that we defeat it."

"Even if doing what you think is right requires you to break the law, like how colored people break laws protesting and marching?" Crackers shot back, not hiding his disagreement with yesterday's march.

Ignoring the word colored, Rosa replied, "Yes. Civil disobedience is a deliberate, nonviolent refusal to obey a law or rule because it violates your convictions. I have mixed feelings about civil disobedience because I believe it's wrong to intentionally break a law when there are provisions within our legal framework to challenge it. I also feel the breaking of one law encourages disrespect for all laws. However, the wheels of democracy turn slowly when change causes discomfort to those in power. Laws are written to protect the general welfare of society and thus reflect the values of the majority. This isn't wrong. However, when a law violates the rights of those outside mainstream thinking, it's every citizen's responsibility to disobey it because, as Gandhi said, 'In matters of conscience, the law of the majority has no place.' The belief that it's my duty to obey a law while working to change it is illogical. It assumes it's acceptable to ignore a principle for a short time. There's no difference between violating a principle for two years, two weeks, two days, or for two minutes. Civil disobedience can be condensed into just four words; 'Not in my name.' From Molly Pitcher to the minutemen farmers to Patrick Henry, Jefferson, and Washington ... each in his or her own way, stood against injustice. Each one looked at the status quo and, in essence, said, I can't be a part of this. I can't, by my actions or my silence, lend my name to this. Instead of obeying the law, they did what justice, reason, and humanity required because they understood that each of us is morally responsible for our actions or inaction. Abraham Lincoln said it well when he wrote, 'To sin by silence when they should protest make cowards of men.'"

Before either of them could ask, Rosa said, "That brings us to what we can do when there is absolutely nothing we can do about something we believe to be unjust. To the universe or God, a whisper is the same as a shout. So, when you can do absolutely nothing else, whisper 'Not in my name,' to yourself and it will be heard where it counts."

Rosa-isms

Doing what's right sometimes generates pain, doing what's wrong always generates suffering.

Don't let what you can't do prevent you from doing what you can do.

People fight so hard to maintain the status quo because they're more interested in their status than your quo.

Curriculum Vitae (The Course of One's Life)

Silence is the voice of complicity.

~Roy Bourgeois

On Saturday, March 14, 1964, after Grant had finished work, Dr. Pierce dropped him off at The Chat-A-Wyle where his mother would pick him up when she returned from visiting her sisters, Tootsie and Betty. As Grant was enjoying his usual raspberry pie buried under two extra-large scoops of chocolate ice cream, Ray Duncan entered the diner to announce that he'd heard on his car radio that Jack Ruby had been sentenced to death for murdering Lee Harvey Oswald.

A week earlier, Grant had read, *A Man for All Seasons*. Then, on Tuesday morning, March 10, Grant finally scraped up the nerve to do something he had thought about doing for a long time. While his classmates mechanically stood and robotically cited their allegiance to the flag, Grant found that remaining seated and silent was far more difficult than he had imagined. Grant knew long before high school that he saw and felt most things differently than did his family, friends, and classmates. Still trying to cope with his growing left-wing, right-brained interpretation of the world, Grant was slowly breaking ranks with those around him who, in his opinion, walked around with eyes glazed over from a daily dose of sterile sameness.

It would also be just as accurate to say Grant's behavior was increasingly a reflection of his disdain for forced conformity, his scorn of anything he viewed as a worthless use of his time, and his growing rebellion against all forms of authority. Sitting silently, Grant wished he could participate in the Pledge, but he could no longer find it within him to continue to invest in something he considered unnecessary, illogical, and silly. More than that, participating in the pledge would be to deny the "Not in my name!" growing within him. It would be another two or three years before Grant would realize he was but one of the millions of boomers who were learning to say, "Not in my name."

It was not until Thursday morning, immediately following his third skipped pledge, that Mrs. MacAllister announced, "Mr. Robinson, would you be so kind as to join me in the hall?" Grant cringed for the second time that morning under the weight of everyone's attention as he stood and slowly walked out into the hall.

The first twenty minutes of each school day was not a regular class. Called homeroom period, it was time set aside for staff to take attendance, get a hot lunch count, hand out report cards and progress reports, and remind students of upcoming events such as yearbook pictures, home games, and deadlines for various assignments. There were also the principal's morning proclamations over the public address system. For many, those few homeroom minutes also provided time to compare and/or copy each other's homework assignments. However, the Pledge of Alliance to the flag preceded all of these activities. Earlier that morning, after filling the cafeteria for their homeroom period, the Class of '64 focused upon Grant when Mrs. MacAllister quipped, "Well if it isn't Mr. Robinson blessing us with his presence," as Grant reported late again. Grant knew she wasn't really angry with him and that she was sending him a message, "Get to class on time and avoid future embarrassment." Mrs. MacAllister was right; Grant was cringing yet again as he passed the two Cool Tables, the Elite Table, and the Loser Table on his way to his seat at the Semi-Nerditude Table.

Outside in the hall, Mrs. MacAllister, who could put the spur in your moment faster than anyone Grant knew, was looming over him with an expression resembling an approaching cold front. "What's with you? Today was the third day you didn't participate in the Pledge. And don't give me one of your 'I don't know what you're talking about looks.'"

Although he had known for three days this confrontation would come eventually, it still felt like a pop quiz he wasn't prepared for as his practiced response melted into a blurted, "Because ... because it's a silly waste of time."

Mrs. MacAllister and Grant were two of the thirty-five-member congregation of the St. James Episcopal Church in Benign. As an acolyte, Grant had helped prepare the elements of Mrs. MacAllister's Holy Communion many times. Grant liked and respected Mrs. MacAllister. Among her many gifts, she was so good at creeping up on you that Grant was convinced she wore a pair of stealths, the product of some secret military research. Regardless, she was his all-time favorite teacher, his current English Literature teacher, a good friend of his mother, and the source of several of the classics Grant had been reading. Although Mrs. MacAllister had moved the fifteen miles from Benign to Redwood following her husband's death, Grant's mother continued as her housekeeper. Each Wednesday evening Grant would go with his mother to Mrs. MacAllister's home to exchange the books she had lent him for more. Next to the Benign Village Library and the high school library, Mrs. MacAllister had the most extensive book collection Grant had ever seen. Not only did she have stacks of books in the basement, but her living room walls also had bookshelves from the floor to the ceiling.

Grant's refusal to participate in the daily ritual may have been ill-advised, but it was not an impulsive decision. Rather, it was a preconceived, calculated protest with a narrow and personal agenda. That, however, was not helping him much at the moment. Grant was glad Mrs. MacAllister had taken him into the hall to question him without the weight of his classmates' stares on a backbone already threatening to buckle under the pressure of the infamous MacAllister evil eye. Among his peers, her withering gaze was well known for its ability to wilt flowers. Besides, Grant knew she had flying monkeys and wasn't afraid of using them.

"You think pledging allegiance to your country is a silly waste of your precious time?"

Grant winced, immediately realizing the words "silly" and "waste of time" weren't a good beginning. He knew he had to be careful not to get her so angry she would stop listening to him.

"I think reciting the Pledge every day is unnecessary," Grant said softly, trying to find his voice admit the sound of his heart pounding in his ears.

"Oh? Would you be so kind as to enlighten me?" she asked, her voice reminding him of Lava Soap as it came at him like a hot, southwest wind from the far corners of hell. An imposing figure at six foot three inches, she was a full five inches taller than Grant and immaculate in every way. Her clothes were the nicest and no doubt most expensive he'd ever seen. They were what regular clothes prayed to look like. Looking up at her, Grant was sure he felt himself getting shorter. Regardless, speaking slowly and looking directly into her unclouded blue eyes, Grant replied just as he had rehearsed it. "I've pledged alliance to the flag hundreds of times, and I meant it every time. I should not have to repeat it every morning because it doesn't wear off overnight. Besides, the right of free speech includes the right to remain silent."

Although Grant's use of the words "remain silent" was a small red flag in the back of her mind, Mrs. MacAllister ignored it as she replied, "No one has suggested it wears off. We repeat the pledge daily to reaffirm our allegiance and we stand together to do so as a public statement of that allegiance. Many of the oaths and pledges we take in life; we take in front of others. Even couples getting married stand in front of their families and friends."

Seeing the briefest of smiles, Mrs. MacAllister instinctively knew Grant had come prepared. Before she caught her next breath, Grant seized the opening. Weakly, but determined, Grant asked, "Did you and Mr. MacAllister repeat your wedding vows every morning?" Although there was a nervous quiver in his voice and despite his boldness, Mrs. MacAllister was more amused than surprised by Grant's willingness to look her in the eye and go toe to toe with her.

Grant expected a rebuttal, a lecture, or, in some way for her to put him in his place. Mrs. MacAllister wasn't one you smarted off to, regardless of how much she liked you and your mother. Everyone knew you didn't cross Mrs. MacAllister, which is why, outside of her hearing, Grant called her "Rubicon." However, with eyes that could pick your pockets, she looked at him for several seconds, a smile lurking at the corners of her mouth. Ignoring Grant's expertly played gambit, she said, "You read it, didn't you?"

Grant didn't have to ask, "Read what?" He knew exactly what she meant. She was referring to *A Man for All Seasons*, a new play by Robert Bolt.

"Yes," Grant said softly, knowing he wasn't out of the woods.

Mrs. MacAllister had loaned Grant the play a week earlier, knowing he would love it. What she hadn't considered was Grant putting it into action, at least not so soon. Although Mrs. MacAllister was no spring chicken, she was still an extremely attractive woman whose persona took over any room she entered. Many of his classmates looked out for her, but most, like Grant, looked up to her. Until that moment, she'd always shared a warm smile when talking to him. The sparkle in her eyes remained, but her smile had faded, not out of anger, but concern. "I don't agree with you on this, but I understand. You know there will be consequences, right?"

Grant nodded. "Yeah."

"You've got pluck; I'll give you that," she said as she took a packet of yellow hall passes from her skirt pocket. She scrawled "Mac" near the bottom of one pass but didn't fill it out. Handing it to him, she said, "You can go now or the first thing tomorrow morning. If you decide to say the Pledge with us tomorrow, you can throw that away."

Grant understood Mrs. MacAllister was allowing him to reconsider his position. He also knew that despite disagreeing with him, she would also be a little disappointed in him if he didn't use the pass. After all, she was continually admonishing her students to "Step outside tribal thinking" and "You weren't born to sing another's song." Besides, like all Robinsons, Grant didn't believe the quality of a decision to be in direct proportion to the time and effort put into making it.

Mrs. MacAllister knew Grant was different by default, not design. She also knew what he had yet to learn, that there were forces within him he did not understand and could not yet control. As they returned to the cafeteria, Mrs. MacAllister softly said, "Remember, it's called, '*qui tacet consentire.*'"

Grant nodded his understanding, before returning to his seat at the Semi-Nerditude Table knowing that, by the end of the week, he might be sitting at the "Troubletude Table." As shy as Grant was, he realized it was not going to be easy for him to step outside the comfort of his classmates' approval and the security of the school's rules, but then, he also knew that getting into trouble was often an acceptable price for standing behind the decisions he made.

Although she had the well-dressed, well-rested look of a Republican, it wouldn't be until he'd completed his first year of college that Grant would learn that, as much as anything he had in his favor that morning, Mrs. MacAllister's politics were anything but those of a conservative.

MacAllister-isms

As long as you concern yourself with what others think of you, they own you.

Spend yourself in worthy causes.

Tap the power of your own fire.

Face life any way you want, except timidly. Don't die of cold feet.

Idealism will get you to the table, but it's not the bread.

You can't be both an eagle and a pack mule.

The Cafeteria Tudes

tude - A Latin suffix meaning state, quality, or condition of

The Indian River Central Class of '64 pecking order was engrained early and deeply by the end of their freshman year and rigidly reinforced throughout their high school years. Some managed to move up a level because of developing athletic ability or being a late bloomer in the looks department, but they were few and far between. Just as water seeks its level, Grant's classmates, with rigid strictitudeness, had remained socially stagnant. This was nowhere better displayed than in the cafeteria.

Grant viewed high school as a blanket of frustration, missteps, torturous boredom, generalized paralysis, inordinate self-doubt, low self-esteem, flagrant lassitude, malevolent mockery, and behavior characterized as being between shameful and shameless that couldn't be kicked off. As a result, he spent hours of his lunchtime observing and identifying what he and Crackers, whose mind reminded Grant of an unmade bed, called the cafeteria tudes.

The nerditudes, although similar, were not to be confused with the jerkitudes. By and large, the nerditudes were friendly, gentle kids who lived more in their heads than in reality. This was the group with which Grant most closely identified, although he also considered himself a solitude with pronounced levels of ineptitudeness.

Jerkitudes, however, weren't particularly nice or gentle. Although they possessed noticeable levels of nerdituteness, they justifiably sat at the table next to the loseritudes, kids continually in trouble and likely to drop out or be kicked out of school as soon as they reached sixteen. There was also a small splinter group of loseritudes that Crackers called the dickitudes, those with extremely high levels of badassitudeness.

Badassitudeness wasn't necessarily a negative quality. It was a most desirable trait for the jockitudes. It was also a defining quality among teacheritudes, those teachers known for their strict discipline. Those teachers without it were limpitudes.

Cheerleaders were known for their pulchritudeness and sat together at the lustitude table. The sexually active girls were slutitudes; the sexually active boys were studitudes. The smartitudes were those with pronounced levels of both aptitudeness and attitudeness.

In a democracy, dissent is an act of faith.

~**William Fulbright**

The dissenter is every human being at those moments of his life when he resigns momentarily from the herd and thinks for himself.

~Archibald MacLeish

Grant was a little surprised when none of his classmates, except for Meredith, his best friend, asked why Mrs. MacAllister had taken him into the hall. Grant didn't give him an answer, other than saying it was all a misunderstanding, because he believed, as did his father and grandfather had before him, that it was not his place to convert others to his way of thinking. Rather, each must come to terms with the world according to his or her own wits, or, as his grandfather would say, "Everyone has to pound their own nails."

The next morning, after attendance, Mrs. MacAllister silently nodded as Grant, yellow hall pass in hand, quietly slipped out the back of the cafeteria on his way to the principal's office. A minute later, he was sitting on the "Group W Bench," while he waited for Mr. George Bush, the principal, to summon him.

As he took a seat in one of the uncomfortable chairs, Grant knew he would have a several-minute wait. Grant understood the strategy behind both the chairs and having students "cool their jets" before being summoned into the inner sanctum of the principal's office. Nervous, more from disliking confrontation than the prospect of being in trouble, Grant was combating the hollow, sinking feeling in his belly. When Mr. Bush, standing in the doorway to his inner office, finally called his name, Grant took a deep breath and murmured, "Why the hell am I doing this?"

In his late fifties, with labored breathing and yellow cigarette stains on his fingertips, time and aging were conspiring against Mr. Bush. There were rumors he was battling cancer, diabetes, Crohn's Disease, and any number of other diseases, all of which were untrue. He had what Grant called a listening gaze as if his eyes and ears were interchangeable. Extremely attentive, his eyes never looked away as he listened so intently you would think his ears were starving for words for his mind to digest. Watching him close his office door behind them with vertigo-inducing slowness, Grant was convinced he had a flask of laudanum in his desk and an anal thermometer in his pocket. Mr. Bush then politely asked Grant to take a seat.

This was not Grant's first visit to Mr. Bush's office, nor would it be his last. More nervous than frightened, Grant sat in the second of the three chairs. As Mr. Bush took his seat behind his large, oak desk, Grant had the presence of mind to note how he was using his desk as a symbol of his authority. He also noticed that Mr. Bush's chair was higher than the others, allowing him to look down on anyone sitting across from him. Grant suppressed a brief urge to smile, as he wondered why he had not noticed any of this before.

Grant liked Mr. Bush more than most students liked their principals. Not only had Mr. Bush always been honest and fair with him, but he'd also always impressed Grant by being more interested in understanding a student problem and working to find a solution than in using his authority as a club. Grant wondered if that was about to change.

Grant was not surprised to discover that Mrs. MacAllister had not given Mr. Bush a head's up on why she had sent him to the office. Of all the lessons she would teach him,

Grant would forever remember the importance of letting people tell their own stories. Mr. Bush listened attentively while Grant explained his position. When he'd finished, Mr. Bush asked Grant a couple of clarifying questions before he said, "It's a sad state of affairs when a high school senior refuses to pledge alliance to his country. I am distressed and disappointed in you, especially since you are a member of the Future Teachers of America Club. I'm not sure what to do with you, but I want you to understand that the school has … that I have the right to force you to say the Pledge."

"With all due respect, Mr. Bush, you have the power to force me to say the Pledge, not the right," Grant clarified somewhat sheepishly, trying to walk the line between being assertive without being argumentative. Grant knew that here was where a smart kid would now shut the hell up, but he had come prepared to present his case and wasn't going to back down. He continued with, "In 1940 the Supreme Court ruled that public schools could compel students to say the Pledge. That's what gives you the power, but no amount of power can make a wrong thing right."

Mr. Bush, with just a hint of anger in his voice, said, "You've proven you know how to use an encyclopedia and have the moxie to walk in here; now show me you have the smarts to be quiet and listen." Then Mr. Bush pointedly explained that he knew all about his powers and from where they came before launching into a description of Grant's lack of any rights. Then, with unsaid thoughts still on his tongue, he suddenly stopped. Perhaps he remembered that two years earlier, Grant had refused to sign a pledge that he would not cheat on World History tests. Perhaps Grant's expression told him there was nothing left to say that would change Grant's mind.

Grant didn't know then just how fortunate he was to have had so many intelligent, understanding mentors during his high school years. Mr. Bush could have, as Grant expected, shut down the debate, given Grant detention or some other punishment, and snuffed out Grant's mini-rebellion. He didn't. Rather, he sat back in his chair and asked, "As a future teacher, what would you do if you were me?"

"I'd shoot myself," Grant thought. However, rather than his reflexive response, Grant shrugged his shoulders, and mumbled, "I don't know." Besides, his first from the hip response to Mr. Bush's question was not a reflection of his true feelings about him.

"That's an intriguing answer, but not very enlightening," Mr. Bush replied in an attempt at sarcasm, something, to his credit, he'd never mastered with students. "You don't get to ignore school policy and then pretend you're the victim when it's time to face the consequences," Mr. Bush told him as he stood and walked to the door. "I'll be back in ten minutes and when I return, I expect you to have both a proposal and rationale to support it." The closing door corresponded with Grant murmuring, "Shit!" under his breath.

For the first few minutes, Grant sat stunned and confused. He had not expected to be taken seriously, let alone having to clean up his mess. Then, slowly, Grant began to like the idea of playing a role in deciding his fate. Grant was destined to spend a lifetime challenging authority and that morning's lessons would become invaluable. First, if he didn't take himself seriously, neither would anyone else. Second, always provide the opposition with a face-saving way of agreeing with you.

"So, what am I to do with you?" Mr. Bush asked after he closed the door and sat on the edge of his desk, looking down at Grant. What he didn't tell Grant was that he had used the time to call Grant's father. From Mr. Bush's perspective, the call had not gone well when Stanley told him, "I can't help you. This is my son's pile of wood to stack."

"I think I should spend homeroom period in the hall outside the cafeteria until after the Pledge. Everyone will think I'm being punished for something, but won't know what," Grant offered as a solution.

"Until you tell them," Mr. Bush said without any indication of how he felt about the proposal.

"I won't say anything because I don't care if anyone else says the Pledge or not."

"Okay, what's your rationale?"

Mr. Bush listened with interest and then amusement as Grant equated his position with that of Sir Thomas More of England. Grant began by again stressing he was not opposed to the Pledge, only to his having to repeat it daily. He then explained why More had been imprisoned and later executed for refusing to sign an oath that included accepting King Henry VIII's claim to be the supreme head of the Church of England. At his trial, More's defense had been based upon his having remained silent regarding the oath and that, under the law, silence construes consent, not descent. Grant stunned Mr. Bush when he quoted a few lines from Robert Bolt's play from memory. "The maxim is *qui tacet consentire*. The maxim of the law is 'Silence gives consent.' If therefore, you wish to construe what my silence betokened, you must construe that I consented, not that I denied."

Far from being angry, Mr. Bush was almost laughing as he said, "So your position is that not reciting the Pledge means the same as saying it?"

"Not to others, but to me, then yeah it's the same," Grant replied.

For the remainder of his senior year, Grant left his morning homeroom class after attendance to stand in the hall during the Pledge. He never told anyone why, nor did anyone ask. His protest was indeed private. Mrs. MacAllister would occasionally permit herself a knowing smile when she called his name, but she never mentioned the incident again. Several months later, she signed his senior yearbook with, "Grant, you have a keen mind and, because I believe you will be successful in whatever you attempt, I pray you will use your gifts for good rather than ill. The path before you will not be easy for you or those who love you, but I have little doubt that you will be happier than most. Remember, it isn't what they call you; it's what you answer to. Best Wishes, Mrs. Mac."

At the end of the year, following the graduation ceremony, Mr. Bush shook Grant's hand and, with a wide grin, said, "I'm going to miss our talks, but not very much." Later, while standing with his parents, Mrs. MacAllister walked up to shake Stanley's hand and to hug Maretta. Then she turned to Grant saying, "If you ever need a friend, there's a warm ear and a cold Cream Soda waiting for you in Redwood." Little did Grant know, following a lackluster first year at college, just how valuable a friend he had in Mrs. MacAllister.

Rosa-isms

Being true doesn't automatically make it good to say.

Assuming authority will be grateful for you telling it the truth is like assuming short people are better at miniature golf.

Authority seeks to make questions sound like answers and having done so, it then seeks to turn those answers into weapons.

Think twice, Grant, often three times, before keeping your mouth shut lest your thoughts break out into words.

There's a difference between sticking your neck out and keeping your chin up.

Monday, January 6, 1964 - Walk Like a Man

I was just too stubborn to ever be governed by enforced insanity.

~Bob Dylan

Grant's last class on the first day back from his senior year's Christmas Break was Mr. Montford's Mechanical Drawing class. Mr. Montford would often crack a joke or two during class and that day it was no different. Several minutes into the class Mr. Montford asked, "Okay, who knows what John-John got for Christmas?"

To Grant, any joke about President Kennedy's small son was not appropriate or amusing less than two months after his father's death. However, this one was especially disgusting. With a big smile, Mr. Montford delivered the punch line, "A Jack-in-the-box."

Grant just sat there, stunned into silence as his anger built. After some nervous chuckles, everyone went back to work. However, Grant could not let this insult to the fallen president go unchallenged as he murmured, "Not in my name."

A few months earlier, Frankie Valli had released the song, "Walk Like a Man," with the chorus lyrics, *Walk like a man/Talk like a man/Walk like a man my son*. An instant hit, the song was still getting a lot of airtime on the radio.

Mr. Montford had an unusual gait, just short of a limp, about which he was somewhat sensitive. Everyone has, by law, the right to remain silent, but only the smart ones do so. That day, Grant wasn't smart enough to exercise that right. A few minutes after his distasteful joke, as Mr. Montford walked across the front of the classroom, Grant called out, "Hey, Mr. Montford, you walk like a man. Do you do any other impersonations?"

Heads turned, eyes widened, and mouths fell open as his fellow students looked back and forth between Grant and Mr. Montford. Grant, who in class made fewer waves and less noise than a fish, had stunned everyone by stepping so far out of character. Giving him a look like Grant had just evicted his mother, Mr. Montford's neck and cheeks turned cherry red on their way to a nice burgundy."

In 1964, such insults earned a student a one- or two-day suspension. If the entire class had not started laughing, Mr. Montford might have settled for giving him one of his famous "ass chewings" in the hall. Instead, after staring at Grant with a mixture of anger and surprise, he slowly walked to his desk, sat down, and began to write. There were no doubts in anyone's mind that Grant had gone too far. Except for Grant, who began packing up his books, it was pin-dropping silent in the room. With what had to be a tremendous amount of tongue-biting restraint, Mr. Montford, looking at Grant said, "Come here, please."

Grant, his books in hand, stood in front of Mr. Montford's desk as he finished writing both a pass to the principal's office and a note explaining Grant's rude and disrespectful behavior. As the silence got deeper and louder, Grant wondered if anyone could hear his heart pounding. More afraid of what his parents would say than of what the principal would do, Grant's anger and indignation began to melt into a puddle of second thoughts inside his belly.

"You know the drill," Mr. Montford said as he handed Grant the note and pass.

Grant could feel the weight of his classmates' eyes following him toward the door. Everyone knew that Mr. Montford's cold, silent demeanor harbored a hot, raging temper that, like a genie in a bottle, would erupt whenever someone rubbed him the wrong way. This wasn't the first nor would it be the last time Grant, who housed a hot temper of his own, would challenge authority in the heat of the moment. By the time he graduated from college, Grant would come to believe it was everyone's civic duty to mistrust and question authority. This wasn't new for Robinsons; a distrust of authority ran in their veins, each corpuscle containing the belief that authority lies with equal measures of malice and stupidity.

Folded once, the note would have been easy for Grant to read, but he was too busy taking deep breaths and wondering what to say to Mr. Bush. Although Grant had had his share of "talks" with him, Mr. Bush had grown to enjoy seeing him enter the outer office with a yellow hall pass in his hand. No two visits had been for the same offense. After several minutes of sitting in one of the hot seats," Grant heard Mr. Bush say, "Send in Mr. Robinson."

To Grant, Mr. Bush looked more like a circuit-riding preacher than a principal as he silently read Mr. Montford's note. Finally, after letting Grant stew in the juices his temper had heated to the boiling point, Mr. Bush laid the note on the desk in front of him. "Now and then, Grant, you act as if stupid is its own reward. Did you read this note?"

"No," Grant replied truthfully.

Mr. Bush seemed surprised as he asked, "Why not?"

"It wasn't written to me."

Although he knew Grant well enough to believe him, he said, "But it's about you."

Grant didn't reply.

"Do you want me to read it to you before I ask you to explain your actions?"

"I don't care," Grant answered just loud enough to be heard.

"Perhaps not caring is part of your problem. So, tell me what happened."

"I told Mr. Montford he walked like a man and asked him if he did any other impersonations."

It was obvious from his expression that Mr. Bush wasn't familiar with the song. It was also obvious he wasn't amused. "Why would you say that? Don't you like Mr. Montford?"

"I like him fine," Grant said as he began to find his voice.

"Being argumentative is nothing new for you, but being rude and disrespectful is," Mr. Bush said as he lowered his chin enough to be able to look at Grant over his dark-rimmed glasses. Then he leaned back in his chair with his elbows on its arms and his fingertips touching, forming the top of a triangle. Finally, he said, "You're bright enough to understand this kind of behavior won't be tolerated. You are looking at a day's suspension here. Is that what you want, staying home for a day?"

"No."

"I don't think your parents would approve of that, do you?"

"They don't approve of much I do."

Mr. Bush looked up at the clock before reading the note yet again. Then he said, "You can take this note back to Mr. Montford and apologize to him in front of the class or you can take home a discipline notice informing your parents you have a one-day suspension."

It wasn't a difficult decision. Being embarrassed and humiliated in front of his friends as he apologized to Mr. Montford was far better than having to explain his actions to his parents. Besides, he knew what he'd said required an apology. What Grant didn't know at the time, and wouldn't know for another three years, was that Mr. Bush had let him off easy because he hadn't offered any excuses for his behavior nor had he said a word regarding Mr. Montford's Jack-in-the-box joke. Grant's father had taught him well. Grant didn't mention Mr. Montford's crude joke because that was Mr. Montford's water to carry.

As he walked toward his waiting humiliation, Grant thought, "Meredith is right, if you can't catch hell for it, it's not worth doing."

It would later be ironic that Mr. Montford would be the first teacher to send Grant to the principal's office in the seventh grade and, six years later, be the last to send him to the principal's office in his senior year. Even more ironic, during his sophomore year of college, Grant and his girlfriend would go on a double date with Mr. Montford and his new fiancé, one of Grant's college classmates.

We each write the terms of our surrender

You control your words until you say them, then they control you.

Being right doesn't necessitate proving another wrong

It's called "expressing an opinion" because of the speed at which you give it.

If your kind of honesty isn't kind, it's the wrong kind.

To the thrower, an insult is a dart. To the receiver, it's a spear.

The truer the insult, the harder it is to laugh off.

Crossing the Rubicon

She was my favorite teacher, not for filling me with answers, but with questions.

~Grant Robinson

One year and six days after his high school graduation, Grant's stomach felt like knotted Jell-o as he crossed her front porch to ring the bell. Five days after completing his first year of college, with new knowledge dripping off him, he heard, "Come on in, Grant, it's open," from the other side of the darkened screen door.

Knowing his mother had told her he'd finished his freshman year with a GPA of 1.8 only added to his nervousness. And although he'd talked briefly to her at church on Sunday, looking her in the eyes wouldn't be easy. However, to his relief, she greeted him with a warm hug, an even warmer smile, and as promised, a cold bottle of cream soda. Not one for small talk or polite chatter, Mrs. MacAllister immediately launched into an hour's worth of questions about college. "What do you love about college? What would you change about your first year? What was the best decision you made? What surprised you the most?" Those were followed by, "What books did you read? What inspired you? What stretched you? In what ways do you see the world differently now? What did you believe a year ago that you no longer believe? What new ideas set you on fire?"

Grant had expected her to "give him hell" about his GPA, but she didn't mention it until, three cookies and two Cream Sodas later. Just before he left, she told him, "I've got nothing to say about your grades that you don't already know. You also know what you need to do about it." Then she gave Grant a parting hug. As he started down her porch steps, she called to him through the screen door, "By the way, for what it's worth, of all the nicknames I've been given over the years, 'Rubicon' is my favorite."

Headed home, Grant smiled as he wondered how she knew about the nickname. He also wondered what his former classmates would say if he told them about getting hugs from Mrs. Mac. However, those hugs were far too special to share.

MacAllister-isms

After you leave college, Grant, remembering why you went.

There's no better set of blinders than a set of beliefs.

Once you know a truth, you can't un-know it.

Science fiction is a refuge for ideas waiting to be accepted.

A classroom isn't a receptacle, but a vessel that can only explore if it leaves the harbor.

CHAPTER SEVEN

Wise And Otherwise

After God created the world, Genesis records that, "God saw that it was good." I find it amusing that God when describing the world, he thought it was good and not perfect. Perhaps God looked at the earth and thought, "Close enough for a six-day job." Regardless, if good instead of perfect satisfied God, then good is good enough for me.

Benign Was More Than a Town; It Was a Time.

Benign was a time when you left something better than you found it, comedians made you laugh without being vulgar, and parents taught their kids to pay attention in school because they didn't have the right to waste the teacher's time. It was a time when people traveled to far-off places through the books they got from the local library when you turned off the lights when you left a room, and when newscasters reported the news without their personal spin.

It was a time when "folksy" wisdom came from every direction. Haste makes waste. A chain is only as strong as its weakest link. You can catch more *flies with honey* than with vinegar. If wishes were horses, then beggars would ride free, A closed mouth catches no flies. A watched pot never boils. Then there were the "don'ts." Don't bite off more than you can chew. Don't wish your life away. Don't bite the hand that feeds you. Don't burn your bridges behind you. Don't throw the baby out with the bathwater. And, don't blow your own horn.

Benign

Benign was a time when, instead of handheld computer games, children used their imaginations and creativity playing with Erector Sets, Lincoln Logs, and Fort Apache Play Sets. They played dominoes, jacks, hopscotch, hide and seek, pick-up stix, checkers, Chinese Checkers, paper dolls, Mother, may I?, Red Rover, kick the can, and marbles. They played in sandboxes, shot peashooters, went roller skating, ice skating, flew balsa-wood airplanes and enjoyed homemade kites, stick guns, and slingshots.

Benign was a time when you weren't economically marginalized, you were poor; when you hadn't failed to fulfill your wellness potential, you were sick; when you weren't involuntarily un-domiciled, you were homeless; you weren't experience enhanced, you were old; and when you weren't an incomplete success, you had failed.

Benign was a time when the names Doris Day, Princess Grace, Campanella, Winchell, DiMaggio, Bardot, Liberace, Peron, James Dean, De Gaulle, Marciano, and Einstein were well known. Benign was a time of "Does she or doesn't She", "Good to the last drop", "It takes one to know one", Dennis the Menace, Mickey Mouse, "born on a mountain top", carrying a torch, Mrs. Paul's Fish Sticks, Studebakers, Green Stamps, lightening bug rings, Uncle "Miltie," goody-goody gumdrop, a bug in a rug, monkey's uncle, ant farms, mothballs, two bits for a beer, one potato, two potato, three potato, four, long-hair music, and everyone wondered where the yellow went.

The Second Chance - Saturday, March 25, 2006

"When was the last time you can remember the half-time air being sweet perfume?" T.N. asked Grant.

"Not since my last Dylan concert," Grant chuckled. "Does McLean's 'sweet perfume' refer to the smell of smoking marijuana?"

"Some think so, but most believe it's more likely he was referring to the tear gas used on the protesters at the 1968 Democratic National Convention in Chicago with *the sergeants playing a marching tune*, referring to the police or National Guard marching in formation toward the protesters."

"I always thought that line was about draft sergeants and the marching tune referred to the draft," Grant offered.

"Until McLean tells us for sure, your opinion is as good as any. The beauty of the song is that we can each bring to it what we want."

Grant nodded in agreement before asking, "Following your lead, then those getting up to dance and trying to take the field refers to the protesters trying to protest, and the marching band would be the police or Guard refusing to yield to them."

"Yeah, but there are a lot of people who think it's about the protesters at Kent State and that the Ohio National Guard is the marching band. Then there are those folks who think it has nothing to do with protesters. They think it's about the Monkees."

"The Monkees? As in, 'Hey, Hey, We're the Monkees?'"

"Yeah, the Monkees weren't a real band. They were four actors who auditioned for parts in a television show. They were the 'players' who McLean suggests were trying to replace the Beatles and the Beatles are the 'marching band' who refused to yield to them."

"At least the verse ends well because I have no idea what was revealed the day the music died," Grant said, shaking his head.

Both men were silent for several seconds before T.N. asked, "As I recall, you went through a 'protesting' phase back in high school and into your college years."

"Joan says I never got past that phase and that I'm stuck in the sixties."

"I think I agree with her," T.N. grinned.

"I can't deny it, except I take exception to the word 'stuck.' I prefer to think of it as 'dwelling' in the sixties."

"What, including people, do you feel influenced you most in developing your 'protester-ness?'"

"Ask any Robinson and you hear how it's in the Robinson DNA. However, we aren't protesters as much as we're dissenters. And our 'dissenter-ness,' we believe, comes from our inherent need to question everything ... and everyone. I'm not sure how much of that is genetics or environment. I do know whatever kernel of 'questioning-ness' I entered life with was nourished, first by my father, and then by teachers like Mr. Borcey, Mrs. MacAllister, Mr. Huntress, and Mr. Gilbert. Of course, there was also Rosa, who had more 'questioning-ness' than anyone I've ever met."

"As I recall, you were pretty tight with Mrs. MacAllister."

"I am surprised you knew that. It wasn't something I shared."

T.N. smiled. "You didn't have to. It wasn't hard to tell from the way she smiled at you, even when she was pissed off at you, that Mrs. MacAllister had taken a special interest in you."

"Yeah, and she also liked Dylan."

"I didn't care much for Dylan, but I did like Joan Baez's music and she sure sang better than Dylan."

Grant laughed. "My dad used to say Dylan sounded so bad that deaf people refused to read his lips."

T.N. nodded his agreement. "In college, I had an anti-war poster of Joan Baez and her two sisters sitting on a couch with the words, 'Girls Say Yes to Boys Who Say No.' However, I never found that to be the case."

The Streetlight Incident

Stupidity has a knack of getting its way

~Albert Camus

Grant, a dark-night farm boy two miles from home, wouldn't, had he been asked, have had a single good reason for being in town that time of night. Other than it being a double-dog or perhaps a triple-dog-dare, Grant wouldn't have had an explanation for how the challenge had been translated into that night's reality. Regardless, the hour it took him to complete it fell far short of being his finest. In the center of Benign, at the intersection of Main and Commercial, stood one of six downtown streetlights. To the east, Main Street ended in a rotary in front of the Presbyterian Church. In the center of the rotary was a small island of grass and flowers surrounding a Civil War cannon and a memorial to Benign's fallen in that war. From that memorial, while resting his twenty-two-caliber rifle on the cannon, Grant shot out Benign's most prominent streetlight. At fifty yards, it wasn't a difficult shot, even at nine o'clock on a Saturday night.

He'd paced it off four times the day before, taking time to check and recheck the angles. It wouldn't be enough to hit his target, he had to make sure that his bullet didn't go beyond harmless to anyone downrange. The top floor above Whatchamajiggers Hardware was an empty apartment and the perfect backstop. No one would see a small twenty-two caliber hole in the deteriorating siding twenty feet above the sidewalk.

Grant knew the rifle's report would draw a lot of attention on Benign's busiest night so, dressed in blue jeans and a black sweatshirt, he waited for just the right moment.

However, being in the center of the street with little cover, he couldn't wait long without being seen. His heart pounding as he fought to control his nervousness. He took several deep breaths, feeling the tension in his muscles relax as he slowly allowed each to escape his lungs. He was surprised by how relaxed he was becoming with each passing second, his confidence building until no trace of doubt remained. He knew his target would explode upon impact, just as he was picturing it in his mind.

Ready, he pressed his eye to the scope, slid his finger inside the trigger guide, and slowly took a deep breath and held it. At that moment, nothing else existed beyond the light, his breathing, and his finger as he slowly squeezed the trigger until he sent fifty grams of stupidity into the night. Knowing there'd be too many people around for more than one shot and, if caught, not wanting to have shells on him, Grant had only brought one bullet. At first, he thought he'd missed, but as he calmly hid his rifle in the thick flowers surrounding the base of the cannon, the light bulb drew everyone's attention as it grew brighter and brighter before finally exploding to deposit small flakes of glass on the intersection below. Then, bathed in the resulting darkness, Grant calmly walked north on a nearby side street. Grant had to fight to keep his feet from keeping up with his rapidly beating heart because he knew if he ran for the truck, he'd be noticed and certainly caught.

Halfway to a waiting Yo-yo, Grant heard a car turning at the cannon and onto the street behind him. Before its headlights found him, he moved from the sidewalk to the shadows where he quickly hid behind a circular flower garden located between two houses. He didn't know it was a police car slowly moving up the street until he saw the beam of light searching the shadows. Grant laid flat and face down behind the flowers with his white hands pulled inside his sweatshirt sleeves.

"This guy is good!" Grant murmured as the spotlight slowly swept over and around him. He wasn't sure if he was more frightened or excited as he fought the urge to stand and run. Finally, the car proceeded down the street, stopping every few feet to search the darkness. Then, just short of Yo-yo's parked truck, with Yo-yo crouched low in the seat, the police car turned around and returned, slowly searching the other side of the street. A few yards from where Grant cowered, the officer turned around again, parked, turned out his lights, and waited. From the way the police car was angled, Grant knew escape was only possible by heading back past the officer and away from Yo-yo. Staying in the shadows he weaved his way behind some houses and toward the cannon. It was then, in a better light, that he discovered he was being stalked by a New York State trooper. This wasn't the town deputy or a county sheriff and meant nothing but pure trouble and certain capture. He and Yo-yo hadn't had much of a plan to begin with, let alone a backup plan. Swallowing the urge to run for it, Grant knew he had to slim-chance it by moving southwest toward the now darkened intersection. Behind a dumpster, he took off his sweatshirt, dropped it inside, and entered the intersection between the barbershop and Pearl's Department Store wearing a white t-shirt. He wanted to be seen calmly walking through town.

It was a good twenty minutes before Yo-yo pulled up beside him. With a sigh of relief mixed with disbelief he'd made it, Grant climbed into the cab next to a smiling Yo-yo. Laughing as they celebrated their guy-hood they made the turn in front of Baker's large white house and headed toward the Oxbox Road, they were passed by a State Police car headed in the same direction. Several seconds later they met the same police car headed back toward town as they turned onto the Oxbow Road toward home. Grant watched the police car through the back window and thought he saw the red hint of break-lights as they popped over and behind the hill near the Van Tassel farm. Realizing that the trooper may have recognized the truck as being the one parked down the street from the cannon, Yo-yo scared the hell out of Grant when he yelled, "Hang on! I want to try something!"

Well known for his reckless streak and a good-time grin, when it came to making bad, behind-the-wheel decisions, few had a leg up on Yo-yo. However, what he did next surpassed even Grant's expectations. Before Grant could utter a protest, let alone fasten his seatbelt, Yo-yo turned off his headlights, left the road, and drove at an angle into Van Tassel's cornfield. Although the top of the cab was above the six-foot corn, anything reflecting light was safely out of sight. Seconds later, moving fast, the state trooper came over the hill and passed them, heading out of sight in the direction of their intended sanctuary.

"That was great!" Yo-yo said, pleased with himself as they watched the trooper's lights being swallowed by darkness. Grant was also pleased ... pleased he hadn't wet his pants. Yo-yo then drove them out of the cornfield, and they headed back through town to the Chat-A-Wyle where Yo-yo's mother worked as a part-time cook. Telling her the truck wasn't running well, and with the truck parked out of sight behind the diner, they rode home with her at the end of her shift. The next morning, they picked up the truck before retrieving Grant's rifle from the flowers and his sweatshirt from the dumpster.

Truth and Why

If you seek the truth with an open heart it will find you.

"How have you been? Haven't seen much of you lately," Rosa asked with a warm smile as Grant took his favorite stool at the end of the counter.

"I've been working on a term paper for my philosophy class. We were given two one-word topics to choose from and I chose "truth.""

"Ouch. What was the other topic?"

"Why?"

"That's it; just why?" Rosa asked as she wiped the counter clean before placing a cream coda in front of him without having to ask him what he wanted to drink.

"Yeah. I know more about truth than why, not that I know all that much about truth," Grant chuckled. "Now, if lies were a choice, we'd be playing in my ballpark."

"You can't know a lot about lies without knowing a lot about truth," Rosa grinned. "How long does your paper have to be?"

"He wouldn't tell us, but most everyone says we need at least eight, double-spaced typed pages."

"Since when has what everyone says been of any interest to you?" Rosa teased. "If your instructor didn't specify how long it was to be, there's a reason. Don't worry about the length. Just start writing; the truth will tell you how long it should be. Besides, the more you add to the truth the more you subtract from it."

"I'm beginning to think I should have picked 'why?' I would have but he wouldn't tell us why what? He said we had to figure that out ourselves."

"And that's why he didn't specify the length. It will be different for everyone; there's no right number of pages. The answer to 'why?' isn't all that difficult."

"Now I wish I'd picked it."

Rosa, her hair the color of wisdom, came around the counter and slid onto a stool next to him, something she'd done dozens of times during his high school diner years. "I expect I shouldn't ruin your professor's fun, or yours, but it didn't matter which word you picked. Here's a tip about truth and why. They are the same in that they are each in search of the other."

"What do you mean?"

"I said I'd give you a verse, not the entire chapter," Rosa chuckled as she slid a dime in his direction. "I added the two new Dylan songs to the jukebox."

"Really? Thanks," Grant said as he picked up the dime and headed toward the jukebox. When he returned to his stool, he took out a notebook. Rosa smiled at the pleasure of again seeing Grant doing schoolwork at the end of the counter. She had no idea how many afternoons he'd spent on that same stool doing schoolwork while in high school. After T.N., Grant was by far her most frequent customer. She'd watched Grant enough to know the louder the diner became, the deeper it drove him into whatever he was thinking about. Unlike anyone she knew, noise and confusion seemed to be two of Grant's best friends. She'd watched Grant become better and better at compartmentalizing his mind and not always to his advantage.

"Without giving me the answer, how about another tip to get me started?"

Rosa smiled at him. "Okay, but only one. Smiling, she said, 'You need to learn how far you can push someone.'"

"I think I just did," Grant replied, returning her smile. "But 'Only those who will risk going too far can find out how far one can go.'"

"Very good; I'd forgotten all of the T.S. Eliot Mrs. MacAllister had you read. Okay, smart aleck, for that you've earned two more tips. First, surround yourself with people looking for the truth and get as far away as possible from those who say they've found it. Remember that when you're writing the last page of your paper. Second, when the door between a lit room and dark room is opened, it's the light, not the darkness, that passes through it."

"I think I'm in way over my head here," Grant said softly.

"Wasn't it your buddy, T. S. Eliot, who said, 'If you aren't in over your head, how do you know how tall you are?'" Rosa teased as she left him to greet the couple at the door.

Rosa-isms

The more you stretch the truth the thinner it becomes.

Truth is like a puppy; it will follow you regardless of where you go.

You can't wear out the truth by using it.

The truth would be easier to swallow if it tasted like chicken.

I'm Feeling Glad All Over - Dave Clark Five

You should have agreed with me this morning while you had the chance; I changed my mind this afternoon.

~Brenda

Lloyd Price's 1959 hit, "Personality," was, for Grant, a near-perfect description of Brenda. The girls who didn't hate her wanted to be her, and the boys would have overwhelming elected her best student body president. Around Brenda, boys were one-thought thinkers as their eyes fell in love with seeing her. When she spoke body English, they listened. Brenda never met a sweater she couldn't fill, and the sway of her hips not only put a strut in many a young man's walk, several nearly died of testosterone poisoning. As one of Grant's classmates was heard to utter in the locker room, "Brenda is so fine I'd drink her bathwater."

Although he wasn't immune to the same physiological responses any hormonally enhanced sixteen-year-old boy had around Brenda, Grant wasn't in lust with her. They didn't share the same interests, they didn't have the same friends, and, for the most part, they cordially disliked one another. However, during the last semester of their senior year, they discovered they liked to debate each other for the same reason some people like fencing. They enjoyed crossing swords, sticking it to each other without seriously hurting one another. Grant also discovered Brenda was far different from Amber Camp, an equally well-endowed girl in school.

Grant and Amber Camp (nicknamed Ample Deecup) grew up together. By their junior year, Grant knew she'd go far, and had many times behind her father's tool shed. Besides what Tinker called their "bodacious endowments,"

Amber and Brenda were also very attractive, very bright, and easily owned any room they entered. The major difference between them was that Brenda's identity and self-worth weren't based upon her cup size. While Brenda happily spent her senior year preparing to make something of herself, Amber was happily getting made.

Until Brenda, Grant believed, according to malestream thinking, that large breasts seldom coexist with well-developed brains. Because he expected her to have the brains of a deep-fried Twinkie, it never occurred to him that he'd ever lose to Brenda in a battle of wits. At first, he was surprised, then embarrassed, and finally shocked that a girl he had considered an airhead was kicking his butt in an argument after argument. Being around girls smarter than him was nothing new, but to be outwitted, outfoxed, and outsmarted by a girl nicknamed "the Bod" was, for Grant, somewhere between outrageous and humiliating. It took a while, but as they forged a kind of truce, Grant realized Brenda's company was well worth keeping. And although she didn't know it, she helped forge a crack in Grant's prejudices regarding women. Because Brenda didn't "fit" his stereotype, Grant was confronted with living proof that he needed to reexamine his beliefs. It took a while, but he came to realize his prejudices about women were as demeaning, disrespectful, and bigoted as any other form of prejudice.

Brenda, like Grant, enjoyed having conversations about something more important than the latest school gossip, the next big exam, or the latest Beatles record. Instead, they debated a wide range of topics, from the infallibility of the Pope to the Civil Rights Movement to the Warren Commission Report. Their free-flowing arguments were spontaneous sparring that broke out as often as South

American coupes. Despite the battering his ego took when they were together, Grant felt "glad all over" after each session of what Brenda called "feuding." Of all the notes written by his fellow seniors in his senior yearbook, Brenda's was his favorite. Like her, it was straightforward, humorous, and honest.

> *"Grant, I could wish you good luck, but forget it. We've had fun this year feuding and I do hope you'll succeed in the future, but I don't know as what. Remember me (No doubt you will). As ever, Brenda"*

What It Takes to Be a Teacher

Grant was sitting at the counter in The Chat-A-Wyle one Saturday afternoon filling out college applications, waiting for a fresh-from-the-oven Raspberry Pie to cool. Knowing it was Grant's favorite, along with a couple of scoops of chocolate ice cream, Rosa would either save Grant a slice or bake one for him every Saturday afternoon when he dropped by The Chat-A-Wyle for his pie and ice cream before heading home from work at Doc Pierce's.

"It isn't enough to have a sense of humor, Grant. You also need to cultivate a sense of timing, a sense of fairness, and most importantly, a sense of wonder," Rosa told him.

"What do they have to do with being a teacher?" Grant asked.

"Everything. Your students will respect you if you're fair and fairness isn't a rigid measuring stick, but a flexible measuring tape. Your students will listen if you can make them laugh. But in the end, it isn't about you. If you can teach them to wonder, they'll take it from there. The catch is, you can't teach a sense of wonder, you have to model it." Later that year, Grant's decision to attend the State University of New York at Oswego was, in no small measure, because of Rosa's advice and insights.

CHAPTER EIGHT

Dead Relatives

Benign Was More Than a Town; It Was a Time.

Benign was a time when a parent's, "Because I said so," ended debate on an issue. It was a time when gentlemen didn't swear in the presence of children or women. It was a time when being punished in school paled in comparison to what happened to you when you got home. It was a time when people knew the words to the National Anthem.

Benign was more than a town, it was a time when, if you broke a rule, your word, or a promise, everyone heard it snap. It was a time when children made snow forts and tree houses and when kids had work clothes, school clothes, and church clothes. It was a time back when Spring Break was called Easter and before playing cowboys and Indians was politically incorrect. And it was a time when every boy wanted a dog named Nipper, Tige, or Rin Tin Tin.

Benign was a time when, if you lost your wallet, the person who found it would return it, and you didn't have to open it to know the money was still there. It was a time when, if you ran out of gas, someone would pick you up, drive you to a gas station, drive you back to your car, and a "Thank you," was the only payment they'd accept. It was a time when, if you met people on the street, they'd give you a nod and a smile, directions, a cigarette, a light, or a dime for the payphone.

Benign was a time when we had gray bar hotels instead of correctional facilities, eyes were "peepers," families played Parcheesi together, and bouffant and duck's ass were hairdos. Benign was a time when, "Don't make me stop this car," and "Don't make me come in there," were enough to make any cantankerous child toe the mark.

The Second Chance - Saturday, March 25, 2006

"I think the line about everyone being in one place is about Woodstock. But, what about a generation being lost in space?" Grant asked as they finished their Second Chance lunch.

"I think it's a reference to the popular television show, *Lost in Space*. But some people think it's about the early days of our space program with all of us in one place, in front of our televisions watching Neil Armstrong walk on the moon. Then some think McLean was talking about spaced-out hippies, who many referred to as the lost generation. For many of those hippies, there wouldn't be any time left to start over again."

"This is amazing. I've always loved this song, but the more I'm learning about it, the more I love it," Grant grinned. "So, who is Jack?"

"It could refer to Jack Kennedy and the candlestick could refer to the eternal flame over his grave or it could the Jack in 'Jumpin' Jack Flash,' a song by the Rolling Stones. If so, the candlestick could refer to a Rolling Stone concert at Candlestick Park in San Francisco. Of course, Jack is also a slang term for heroin. Now, have you ever heard of Meredith Hunter?"

"No, I don't think so," Grant replied as he took a sip of his third cream soda.

"In 1968 the Stones hired some Hell's Angels to work security at a concert. During the performance, some of them beat and stabbed Meredith to death."

"I remember that. Isn't that also the night they played a controversial song about the Devil?"

"Yeah. It was called 'Sympathy for the Devil' and many think the lyrics about the flames climbing into the night and the sacrificial rite' refer to the sacrifice of Meredith Hunter. And Satan laughing in delight may well be directed at Jagger who continued to sing and dance as Hunter died."

"Was the girl who sang the blues Janis Joplin?" Grant asked.

"I think so because her nickname was Lady of the Blues. I've read the most popular interpretation of the verse about a woman being asked about some happy news, but the woman only smiled and turned away, is Janis refusing the requests of her friends to stop using drugs and her then dying from an overdose."

"So, who were the children screaming in the streets?"

"I'm not sure. Perhaps they are the young people in the streets of Chicago during the 1968 Democratic National Convention or maybe the college kids at Kent State."

"And who were the father, son, and the Holy Ghost?" Grant asked.

"Many think McLean was referring to Jack Kennedy, Martin Luther King, and Bobby Kennedy. Others believe because McLean attended Catholic schools, that it's the Trinity of God, Jesus, and the Holy Ghost. However, I think it's another reference to Holly, Valens, and The Big Bopper. As for them leaving for the coast, going west into the sunset is symbolic of dying," T.N. answered.

They ate in silence until Grant said, "This place sure brings back a ton of memories. I can almost see Rosa standing behind the counter as if it were yesterday."

"What makes you think she's not?"

First Loves Last

No one becomes a complete person as the product of their ambitions free from the fingerprints of help hands.

Dear T.N.,

I smiled at your recent description of Cindy because I also have fond memories of her. Straight from the bosom of the Catholic Church, Cindy went with me in high school but, despite the romantic glow of drive-in movies and dashboard lights, she never went far. She was a complete package, a good head on her shoulders and Disneyland from the neck down. And shortly after I first wrote you, Cindy and I resumed our friendship after a forty-year hiatus.

Several years ago, parked between the road and the natural spring where my father watered our cows, I'd returned to the Oxbow Road farm to roam around in my childhood. The sticky August air was thick enough to make breathing difficult as I closed the car door and climbed the stone fence. My only relief from the heat was the occasional light breeze of the winds of my history whispering in my ear. A hundred yards from the spring and thirty years from the road, I located the trees that once supported a treehouse my brother and I had built. They were larger now and the scars where they'd grown over the nails were the only remaining evidence of past construction. Like the tongue of regret lapping at memory's door, the twisted bark of one tree also carried the only external scars of my first love, the initials C.P. and G. R. carved inside a heart.

I remember the day Cindy walked into our sixth-grade class and sat right down in my heart, giving me my first heartquake. It was love at first sight as newfound hormones whispered her name. It took me days to muster the courage to write her. She wasn't impressed and, giving me a look with no future in it, she read and then wadded my hopes into a small ball. That pattern of writing, reading, and wadding was repeated many times as I taught her about persistence, and she taught me about rejection. Then, after weeks of trying to impress her with my wit and style, our teacher decided to correct our math by having us exchange papers. I was mortified by my failing grade as Cindy, a top student, laid waste to my ego.

After sixth grade, I didn't see much of Cindy until we were reunited in Sam Jones's eleventh-grade math class. Cindy was still a top student and my interest in figures, especially hers, continued to develop. I would go to class early to leave notes on her desk, this time hoping to exchange more than papers. My writing ability hadn't improved any more than my math skills so as I continued to write to her, she continued to read and wad. I knew my only chance with her depended upon her grading me on a curve. I'm not sure if she finally surrendered to my wit and charm or responded out of pity, but Cindy finally agreed to meet me after school at the Benign Library for a math study date. Then, just as things were beginning to add up, her mother called to confirm her suspicions before ordering Cindy to come home.

Although it should be a continuous process, I think making New Year resolutions is valid when it involves self-appraisal, reflection, and renewal. Last year my first resolution was to find and write Cindy. Why, after nearly forty years, did I write her? I had thought about writing her for years, but I didn't because I was afraid of looking silly, afraid she wouldn't answer, and afraid she would. I was also afraid I'd scare her because my reasons for writing were to tell her there's no "use by date" on friendship and that I still admired, appreciated, and cared about her.

Did I scare her? Maybe a little, at least for the time it took her to decide it wasn't a trick to later sell her life insurance or Amway products. I admit I was apprehensive about how she'd respond, but I wrote her because I was far more afraid of her remaining a "but I didn't" in my life. I, therefore, accepted the risks I took because the word happiness comes from the root word "hap" which means chance. Or, as Ray Bradbury wrote, "You've got to jump off cliffs all the time and build your wings on the way down."

After reminding Cindy that she was the first girl I fell in love with, the first girl I kissed, and the first girl to break my heart, I explained that she was also the first keeper of my cares and the first real best friend I ever had. Then, after telling her that she had had a profound impact upon my life, I added, "Now, all these years later, you and I are strangers. Maybe we could chance to change that. I'd like for us to try to get to know the person each of us became. I'd like to know about your family, your career, and your life. In doing so, maybe we'll become friends again. Maybe not. I don't have a recipe for doing this, a plan on how to get there, or more than a vague concept of where 'there' is. I know it sounds like an 'iffy' idea, Cindy, but 'if' is a conjunction meaning 'an uncertain possibility' and it, therefore, seems appropriate that it's the center of l*if*e."

Although the above was proof I'd gotten over my fear of looking silly, Cindy and I had been here before. She and I had a long history of me writing and her reading and wadding. I was pleased she decided not to repeat that pattern this time, especially after I'd explained how her love, friendship, and example had changed my life. She'd taught me a friend is a safe place to think out loud and we could talk for hours. Although she dumped me a few months later for acting like a jerk, I continued to trust her completely. Along with her puppy-warm eyes, infectious smile, free spirit, and loving heart, I admired her strength, her morals, and her character. I can't imagine anyone ever having a better first love.Grant

PS: Some people come into our lives, leave footprints on our hearts, and we are never the same. – Flavia

Salutations Grant,

Although he lived across the road, I only saw Charlie a few times a year. We had a seasonal relationship. It remained dormant all winter, blossomed in the spring, grew during the summer, and cooled again each fall. Each spring Charlie plowed my garden, his way of re-establishing our relationship. Although we easily talked, debated, and argued for hours, we did so only on those rare occasions when our lives intersected at the mailboxes or while mowing the grass along with the differences that separated us.

Charlie was easy to both dislike and admire. Often our time together passed like kidney stones as we strongly disagreed about religion and politics and, to Charlie, everything was either religion or politics. Loving a good argument, Charlie enjoyed pushing, prodding, and poking me until I'd wrap my anger around his name, generating a muffled moan of pleasure within him. I saw Charlie as a narrow-minded redneck, and he viewed me as a born-again liberal. However, we made each other laugh and we made each other think.

I had resolved to stop by Charlie's last spring to ask him to plow my garden, but I didn't. I had resolved to stop by to ask him about the Township's plans to rezone the land behind his house, but I didn't. After hearing he was sick, I was going to stop over to see how he was feeling, but I didn't. When I heard he was in the hospital, I planned to visit him, but I didn't. I then resolved to go see him as soon as he came home from the hospital, but he didn't.

I'm pleased, Grant, that you and Cindy have again opened your lives to each other by risking enough to overcome the "but I didn'ts." I remember Cindy dumping you for acting like a jerk, but believe me, you weren't acting. I think you were right to find and thank her for the ways she enriched your life because to feel gratitude is half the circle, expressing it the other half. However, I'd also remind you that temptation is clever because it often knocks disguised as an opportunity. Therefore, lover-boy, remember that forbidden fruit doesn't spoil until you pick it, that figures may not lie, but they often promise more than they deliver, and that your marriage is a banquet best enjoyed by sticking to the entree and ignoring the side dishes.

Keep Your Center Hard

Although he fed his family from afar as a lumberjack in Canada during the Great Depression and sometimes worked in a foundry after he returned home, my grandfather had the leathered look and hardy heart of an old-time dairy farmer. He preferred a team of horses to a John Deere, a pitchfork to a bailer, and reacted to most news with, "Everything has gone straight to hell since Roosevelt died." He was a quiet spirit; often content to soak in his surroundings until they became a part of him. Wrapping himself in his thoughts, he kept his distance and expected you to do the same. And although long years of hard living had carved a map across his face, they'd also carpeted the locked rooms of his heart with mistrust.

My grandfather always gave you a look that made you think he hadn't yet made up his mind about you. He turned seventy in our hayfield reliving his heyday as a farmer back before The Great War used up the futures of so many of his generation. He frequently visited our small farm, saying he'd come to help. But in reality, he came to revisit those bygone times where his dreams had begun. He wasn't a warm or friendly man, even after you got to know him. His dark eyes held secrets his smile hinted at, but seldom shared, he remembered more faces than names, and he was quick to remind you that everything time gives, it eventually takes away.

In a rare and uncharacteristic attempt at establishing a personal relationship, my grandfather filled my thirteenth summer teaching me how to build a rain-resistant haystack. I can still hear him explaining how to "tie it all together" by overlapping each pitchfork full of hay with the next while keeping "the center hard." "Keep your center hard, Butch, and nothing will get in," he'd tell me over and over again. I helped build several hard-centered haystacks over the following years and he was right. When they were opened months later their centers were as fresh as the summer days they were built.

Our farm had two large meadows connected by a tree-lined lane consisting of a long steep hill beneath a tangled maze of branches. Our hay wagon, when loaded, would barely squeeze beneath their thick canopy. Dennis and I often rode atop the load down this lane, but only behind a strategically placed pitchfork. When done correctly, you can embed the pitchfork in the hay at a 45-degree angle, using it to guide the branches upward and over you. I didn't see how it began, but I watched it unfold like a slow-motion movie. I was flabbergasted when I realized my grandfather, a master at avoiding the branches, was tangled in their grip. As he desperately attempted to climb over them, they held him in place as the wagon slowly passed beneath him. I was so caught up in the unfolding drama and so sure he'd free himself in time, I didn't yell for my father to stop the tractor. What seemed like an eternity took only a few seconds. As the advancing wagon slid out from under him, my grandfather stopped struggling and looked directly into my eyes. As he hung 15 to 20 feet above the ground, he disgustedly accepted his fate with a single word. Still looking at me, "Fuck" was all he said before he disappeared, leaving the branches as empty as we'd found them.

He should have been hurt or at least sore from the fall. He wasn't. Nor was he nearly as angry as my father for my failure to call to him to stop the tractor. I remember the emotions that passed unspoken between the three generations as we slowly returned to the wagon. My father's anger was in reality a product of his fear that his father had been injured. My fear was quickly replaced by the knowledge I'd let my grandfather down by doing nothing to help. Although I was expected to work like a man in the hayfield, all three of us were reminded that I was still just a dumb kid, not yet ready to cross that invisible bridge into the fraternity of manhood.

I can still see the image of my grandfather, hands in his pockets, walking slowly behind our wagon as seventy years of farming faded to black. That day was never mentioned by any of us again because, like our haystacks, our centers were hard, and nothing got in. Nor, as best I can remember, did my grandfather ever return to the hayfield. Just as I was beginning my fight to enter manhood, my grandfather began his fight to maintain his. That afternoon he and I were outsiders, one looking in and the other looking backward. Although he used more four-letter, short-vowel words than anyone I've ever known, fuck had never been one of them. For him, in that instant, it wasn't an obscene utterance. Rather, in a single syllable, he'd cried, "It's over. My time as a farmer has passed." It was also the first time I saw my grandfather afraid. I'd seen fear in his eyes in that split second before his fall. I'd heard it in his voice as he later assured us he was okay. And I'd felt it in his silence as he walked, head lowered, toward a barn on what he knew to be the back curve of his circle.

My grandfather took two falls that afternoon. The first was off a wagon and the second was into a chasm of doubt lined with descending expectations. Although it took him several years to arrive, I believe my grandfather began his final journey toward his death that August afternoon as he brushed himself off, cursing the overhead branches. For most, dying isn't something we do all at once in a last, single act of living. Instead, death is composed of many losses, each to be mourned in their passing. The loss of energy or eyesight or hope or hearing or bodily functions or a loved one or a driver's license or memories or independence or the ability to make basic decisions about our lives are each a death-bringing grief. I believe my grandfather began to die that summer afternoon with the realization that he was no longer strong or agile enough to be a farmer. Or perhaps he began dying the day he made his center hard so nothing could get in. Now, so many summers later, when I think of him, I realize just how many things have gone straight to hell since my grandfather died.

Bits and Pieces

uncle, n. a term used to indicate you've had enough

My Uncle Ted was the black sheep of the family. No one ever spoke about him above a whisper, at least when I was young. The bits and pieces I overheard always involved the same bits and pieces. Uncle Ted was either in jail, in a fight, intoxicated, or in bed with someone else's wife. I loved Uncle Ted stories, but I didn't love Uncle Ted. He wasn't around much and never came to our house unless he wanted to borrow money, usually late at night. Although I often heard bits and pieces the next day, I seldom saw him. My parents wanted to protect me from his bad influence. Whenever I was bad, they would warn me that, if I didn't behave, I'd grow up to be like Uncle Ted. But that's not why I didn't love him.

My earliest memory of my Uncle Ted is of an incident that occurred when I was about five years old. I remember it well because it was the only time he ever played with me. While Uncle Ted was living for free with my grandparents downstairs, my parents rented their upstairs apartment. I remember going down the back stairs to visit my grandmother. She was sitting in the same chair she always sat in while Ted was in the big green chair by the front door, the one he always sat in. At my grandparent's, everyone knew his or her place.

Ignoring my grandmother's warnings to be careful, Uncle Ted told me to run toward him and jump into his arms. I did so several times. On the last jump, at the last second, he moved, letting me crash into the green chair. He wasn't sorry about my tear-filled eyes and didn't pretend to be. All he said was, "Never trust anyone, especially family." Although I never played with him again, that's not why I didn't love him.

Every year our family gathered at my grandmother's for Thanksgiving Dinner. Even after moving to Benign, about twenty miles away, we visited my grandparents nearly every Friday night after buying groceries at the A & P. I loved going there. We spent the evening sitting in our assigned seats, telling and retelling the same old stories. I loved listening to all the stories about the old days and all my old dead relatives. I especially loved Thanksgiving. I loved the big dinner and playing with my cousins. It was the only time the whole family ever got together, except for funerals. We went to a lot of funerals. I liked the funerals because I got to have a big dinner, play with my cousins, and listen to stories about the latest dead relative.

As I got older, the major topics of discussions before each Thanksgiving gathering were always centered on Uncle Ted. Everyone wondered aloud if he'd come if he'd be alone and if he'd bring his wife or someone else's. I didn't care if he came or not because I enjoyed both the stories about him when he didn't and the new stories he'd generate when he did.

I remember my last Thanksgiving Dinner with Uncle Ted. He came alone explaining his wife wanted to stay home. I knew from bits and pieces that he sometimes got drunk and hit her, so I suspected he had beaten her up. On the other hand, I'd also heard (bits and pieces) that she sometimes got drunk and did things with other men for which the rest of the family felt she deserved a beating. Regardless, Ted was quiet most of the day. He didn't even join in on the retelling of the old, dead relative stories. He just sat getting drunk on my grandfather's wine. Grandpa always had a bottle of elderberry wine for Thanksgiving. I thought he bought elderberry because he was old. Sometimes, over the objections of my grandmother, he would give me a sip saying, "A little wine never hurt anyone." I loved my grandfather because, like his wine, he never hurt anyone.

Late in the afternoon, after most everyone had left, we were watching the local news. The lead story was about a woman who blew up her apartment trying to light the pilot light on her gas stove. They said it was a wonder she hadn't been blown to bits and that she was in critical condition in the hospital. As we watched the film of her being carried to the ambulance, they said she had been drinking and was trying to cook a turkey. We thought we recognized the apartment (from the bits and pieces that were left) and the woman on the stretcher. After calling the hospital and confirming it was his wife, Uncle Ted returned to his green chair and poured himself another glass of elderberry wine. He was still sitting there by the front door when our family left. That's when I stopped loving my Uncle Ted. Now, a lifetime later, I know I'm not a bit better than what it takes to make me bitter. Therefore, I plan to forgive my Uncle Ted ... someday.

Burying the hatchet is easier than letting go of the handle.
Don't let the faults of others separate you from their virtues.
Even bad water can put out a fire.

End of Her Rope
suicide, a.k.a. a grave mistake

Upon arriving home safely, my great uncle found a packed suitcase on the front porch and a locked door. After repeated warnings, my great aunt finally kept her promise. My uncle didn't handle it well. A bad temper and alcohol abuse aren't a firm foundation for intelligent judgments. So, after pounding on the door and yelling in the windows, my uncle made his promise and kept it to the best of his ability. He demanded my aunt open the door or he'd go to the barn and hang himself. My aunt either wasn't convinced of his sincerity or, after years of living with an alcoholic, felt she'd reached the end of her rope.

My aunt found him the next morning. He had found a rope, climbed to the top of the haymow, tied one end around a beam and the other around his neck, and jumped into our family history. She found him sprawled on the barn floor with a broken leg. In his anger and drunkenness, he hadn't considered the length of the rope to be an important variable. It would seem that keeping track of details is important, but a preoccupation with loose ends can result in losing sight of the main objective.

I repeated the above story for several years, believing it was true. It wasn't. At least it didn't happen to anyone in my family. According to my father, it's a story he heard about a man he worked with over fifty years ago. If this memory is incorrect, how many of my other memories are also inaccurate? Memories aren't snapshots, but paintings. Although flawed, they give meaning to the present by giving life texture, direction, and organization. As I'm faced with new challenges, I reinterpret my memories to find new meanings. Therefore, freezing them in time by recording them makes it more difficult to manipulate them.

Memories are retouched artifacts that are often more art than fact as I reconstruct them to suit my needs.

CHAPTER NINE

Dare to Matter

Note: *The following is to be read at my memorial/funeral service.*

There's a story about a man who was being chased by a bear when he fell over a cliff. He managed to grab a short vine and hung high above the canyon while the bear laid down to wait for his return. Unable to move up or down, the man felt safe as long as he stayed put. However, each day a mouse came out of its hole to chew on the vine, slowly cutting away at the man's lifeline. One morning, as the bear waited and the mouse chewed, the man saw a beautiful berry growing nearby. Holding the vine with one hand, the man reached out and picked the berry. It was the sweetest berry he'd ever eaten.

Welcome to my graduation ceremony. First of all, relax. If you didn't get the message that this would be an informal send-off and got all dressed up, take a minute to free yourselves of ties, sport coats, shoes, and anything else that will help you feel more comfortable. I understand getting dressed up is a sign of respect for the deceased, but I promise you there are no dead people here today. As I pen this I don't know how death found me. Perhaps I left unwillingly in tangled sheets and a twisted spread or perhaps it was on the open road or a busy street or perhaps I surrendered my outer shell as softly as shadows on the lawn. Regardless, I approached my graduation from this life much like one approaches a blind date, a little apprehensive, but full of hope, expectation, and excitement.

As for the story about the berry, it contains several truths about living. I leave it to you to find which of its truths are seeking you.

Nothing said here today will add or subtract from the sum of my life. We came here, you and I, not to say goodbye, but to seek some measure of closure and perhaps healing. There is a tendency at such ceremonies to over-compensate for the graduate's shortcomings by focusing upon just the good memories. To do so today will disallow the lessons to be learned from my mistakes, frailties, and failings. Although I wasn't as bad as the worst things I did, I wasn't as good as the best things either. Over the days, months, and years to come, especially at family gatherings, I invite and encourage you to keep my life in balance. Do not remember me in the past perfect tense, but rather forgive me any pain I caused you as you share both the negative and positive. Seek to learn from them both, incorporating them into who you are to become better people.

Much of what I possessed will now be given or thrown away as I'll now be needing less and drastically cutting back on my expenses. However, what I was, I've taken with me. And because the best parts of me came from you, you may now feel an empty place inside at my leaving. That may be especially true of you, Joan. We've been each other's light and love for a lifetime. My light has now dimmed, but not my love. Love doesn't say goodbye; it just keeps finding new ways of introducing itself. So, in the meantime, thank you for loving me enough to tell me the truth when the truth's beauty wasn't pretty. Thank you for loving me enough to encourage me to make my own music and to choreograph my own steps. And thank you for loving me enough to teach me not to blame the band for how I danced. Live and love now in the knowledge that because you loved me, I didn't die an unlived life. And in that empty place, nurture the ability to love again. To do so will subtract nothing from what we shared, but only add to it.

To my sons by marriage, welcoming you into our family was easy, loving you easier yet. Thank you for loving and caring for my daughters. I cherished you as I did them. To my friends, thank you for being ladders, lifeboats, and lamps. You made good friends and you made me a better person. You came when you were needed, and I couldn't have asked for more. When God's first laugh echoed across the universe it broke into pieces called angels. My life was full of angels, each generating smiles, joy, and wonder. I expect you here today were among those angels who added to the texture of my life. I believe I'll be looking down on you as this is read. If so, smile with me now because I was looking up to you as I wrote it.

I know it's customary at these gatherings that a few minutes be used to review the honoree's life. Because I haven't the slightest idea of how to best roll the credits on a life lived and loved, let me start by telling you I loved ducks. I also loved leaves, chocolate chip cookies, trains, outdoor concerts, cactus, rainy days, whales, bookstore browsing, warm hugs, folk music, Sunday naps, giant snowflakes, laughter, talking with friends, and Thanksgiving dinner. However, I disliked asparagus, litterbugs, ice storms, cats, squeaky shoes, red lights, eggplant, shopping, pointed sticks, accordion bands, dogs that shed, exercise, and drivers who didn't signal their intentions.

I entered into life in 1946 and, according to my dad, I did it standing up and talking back. I went on to sustain a smart mouth all my life and seldom followed anyone or anything, especially rules. I entered the public school system in 1951 and was a good student until my mind began to wander, sometime during the second grade. Seventeen years into my life adventure I graduated from high school at the very top of the middle third of my class. I then went off to college where I stumbled and fumbled through a four-year teaching program in a mere four and a half years. I attended college for three terms, Johnson's, Nixon's, and Ford's while maintaining a very high C average. Not bad for a kid who didn't learn to read until he was in the third grade.

It was during my first week at college that I met the wonder who would become the center of my life. Joan gave me roots, and then she gave me wings, teaching me to fly by giving my life purpose. It was a simple purpose really, best summed up in the single word, "Matter." So, when you leave here today, if I mattered in your life, hug Joan for anything I gave you came through me from her. The best thing I ever did was to marry Joan and the best thing we ever did was adopt Lynn, Lisa, Lori, and Leann. Each of you girls came as a gift from God and each of you is a source of tremendous joy and pride. I love you with all my heart and you represent the best evidence possible that Joan and I mattered.

I decided to become a teacher in the sixth grade and never considered anything else. That calling came to me early and young. I loved teaching and it loved me back. It nourished and sustained my soul for thirty years. It generated hope in the future, daily introduced me to wonder and joy kept my spirit open to new beginnings, and taught me that the mind is a vessel for exploring and not for storing. Although I received twenty-seven written reprimands during my teaching career, they had a huge party for me when I retired. At least that's what the letter said.

I hope that I graduated from this life still not owning a suit or a gun. I didn't have a favorite color, seldom drank, never smoked, was never found guilty of a felony, and never fired a high-powered rifle at anyone in anger. I was once run over by a car, was once shot with a shotgun, once had a warrant issued for my arrest, was once sued in court, and once saved the life of a drowning man. I was more easily seduced than conquered, lived the life I wanted, didn't own anything I wasn't willing to give away, was harder to please than to satisfy, and everything I had of value I got the heart way. I was irresponsible with money, had cancer (but it never had me), believed the only way to enjoy the game of life was to tear up my scorecard, and sought not to be a dot eager to be connected to a larger picture, but rather to be a leaf seeking to know the tree.

When you leave here today you will head into your future. Great adventures await you regardless of your age. Your future isn't preordained but awaits you to author. God gives us all the canvas, paint, and brushes we need, but leaves it to us to paint our own stories. So, paint with abandon and use every color. I've used up all my future and can't journey with you into what you will create, but I promise to be waiting for you when you finally lay your brushes down.

Regardless of where your life adventure takes you, you'll encounter fear and pain, both dedicated to slowing your growth and limiting your exploration. Do not fight these foes on their terms. You can't defeat them by hiding inside your castle walls, shriveled, and closed, bracing yourself against their siege. Fear and pain are experts at scaling walls. Rather, to conquer these foes, you must lower your drawbridge, saddle up, and ride out to meet them. Armed with humor and faith, you must attack them in the open. It will be then when you're close enough to see your reflection in their eyes, that you will discover your only real enemy.

Your journey may at times be difficult so treat yourself and others gently for abuse and misuse invalidate. Forgive yourselves for your mistakes as soon as possible. Each sunrise is an invitation, and each new day comes with three handles allowing you to use it as a shield, a weapon, or an opportunity. No matter your circumstances, the choice is always yours.

With over six billion people on this planet, you won't have time to wait your turn to be happy. Therefore, let not your afflictions become your crutch. And if you find yourself in the shadows, remember it's because you allowed something to come between you and the light. Also remember that you need not fear the shadows for they are only slivers of night, proof of the light's power to shatter the darkness.

Everywhere you will encounter hurting people seeking your compassion. You will not be able to help them all, but always, always, always move toward the sound of a breaking heart, because if you don't have Jesus in your hands and feet, you don't have him anywhere. Forgive easily and give generously. Our Lord asks us to first give all we can give so that, having done so, God can then teach us to give that which, on our own, we cannot give.

When you allow others to light their candles from yours, it doesn't shorten your candle nor diminish your light. Therefore, when others seek your advice and counsel, surrender it freely as a gentle mirror reflecting their images and not your own. Remember, it is not the function of the candle to be seen but rather to help us to better see everything else.

Your future will come without any lifetime warranties, so go ahead and exceed recommended dosages. Experience extreme temperatures, store in hot, wet places, tumble dry and don't call before you dig. Keep the spark alive by seeking open flames and avoiding old flames. Be responsible for your contents, remove protective coverings, don't watch for falling rocks, advise parental guidance, and keep your swash buckled and your right-protect notch uncovered. Embrace the process of living by becoming the cause in your life, not just the effect.

Everywhere there will be those who will insist you think just like them. In reality, they are insisting you not think at all. Therefore, don't join any organization that takes attendance, endorses candidates, meets on the second Tuesday of the month, holds an annual dance, marches in a parade, sells raffle tickets, has a logo tie tac, wears matching shirts, or whose chairperson has a larger bladder than you.

Just as traffic lights communicate in a specific, predictable pattern, as best you can, consistently use open, honest, direct communication with others. Establish a pattern others can depend upon, signal your intentions, ignore caution signals, and with open arms, willingly yield the right of way to the way of right. Then, as you learn the difference between vision, revision, and division, your view of others will be clearer because you'll come to see them through the window of your heart instead of the mirror of your fears.

Learn to love your work, whatever it may be. Show up, stand out, lighten the load of your coworkers, and make your work a part of who you are instead of something you do between weekends. However, also guard your spare time for there will be too little of it to spare. There are no unimportant days or insignificant hours, and moments melt away unless you fill them with memories.

In your going forth, do not go where you wouldn't take a child, seek the wisdom of elders, and don't confuse cunning with intelligence, intelligence with information, information with knowledge, knowledge with wisdom, wisdom with justice, justice with satisfaction, or satisfaction with cunning. Invest in determining your ideals, decide what you believe, then strive to live them while wearing your philosophies lightly enough to not exclude the consideration of new ideas and possibilities. I have no clear picture of what Heaven will be like, but I expect to find the path leading up to its gates to be lined with discarded doctrines.

You will also encounter the hands of hate, most often wearing the gloves of indifference. Too often the black hats will win. Get over it. However, when you find people battling against bigotry, prejudice, injustice, or ignorance, join them in their fight. If you cannot find such a fight, start one. Become the good you are seeking in the world.

Seek not to be all things or any one thing. Cherish your inconsistencies. Seek a balance between the opposing forces within you. Each has its value. Balance your dark side with a steady supply of light, your hardness with a softness easily broken, your pettiness and smallness with a largeness of spirit, your shallowness with a deep appreciation of life, your rapid lifestyle with a calm center, and your need to dominate with a desire to serve. William Arthur Ward said it well when he wrote, "The adventure of life is to learn. The goal of life is to grow. The nature of life is to change. The challenge of life is to overcome. The essence of life is to care. The secret of life is to dare. The beauty of life is to give. The joy of life is to love!"

Avoid those who disparage others, who shun effort, who denigrate striving, and who malign searching. Lift up humanity by seeking the truth and in your seeking, overrule more objections than you sustain. Render what you must to age without surrendering the youthfulness within you. Each of us is given, by God, a life sentence to serve. God sent you here to enrich the world, to add to its vision, to deepen its hope, and to serve. Service is the key to unlocking a life that matters. As you seek to serve others, remember that service without faith is crippled and faith without service is blind. Albert Schweitzer was a renowned humanitarian, theologian, missionary, organist, and medical doctor. Many of you are too young to remember him but his life was a living testimony to his words when he wrote, "I don't know what your destiny will be, but one thing I know; the only ones among you who will be truly happy are those who will have sought and found how to serve."

Now, as you begin your futures, cast off your lines and leave the harbor. Sail beyond boundaries and traditions, don't trust the winds of authority or popular thought, chart your course, and let your eyes fall in love with seeing. And when the winds abandon your sails, when there is no one to draw you near, or when the night is so black you can't remember sunlight's warmth, remember it's okay to pray while you row. And if you must seek shelter from the storm, seek it behind a wall of friends.

I once purchased a new used blue Chevy. I'd owned it for less than a month the first time I parked it at the mall. Because I rarely locked anything, I was surprised to find it locked when I returned with my purchases. I was also surprised when my key wouldn't unlock it. Because I had three sets of car keys, I assumed I'd selected the wrong one. In attempting to unlock it with a second key,

I inadvertently broke it off inside the lock. Disgusted, I contacted mall security. Within minutes a security officer arrived and quickly unlocked my new used blue Chevy using a long, thin piece of metal he carried in his van.

As the officer drove away with my appreciation and a two-dollar tip, I attempted to start my car. The ignition key wouldn't work. As I again checked to see if I was using the right key, I noticed some magazines on the front seat. It was then, as I realized the magazines weren't mine, that I realized the car wasn't mine either. The fact that my car was the same make and color didn't ease my embarrassment for having tipped a security officer two dollars for helping me break into someone else's car. It didn't take me long to find my car. It was parked two spaces away. It wasn't locked.

As you travel from here you will encounter many such new used blue Chevies, often disguised as inviting places behind locked doors. Remember that some doors are locked for a reason, that it takes intelligence to open doors and wisdom to know which doors to leave closed, that being able to get there isn't proof you belong there, and that the world is full of those willing to help you make a mistake.

A journey isn't completed until you return home, so I have to go. So do you. I haven't moved beyond you, but rather, it's time for you to now move beyond me. We each have an appointment to keep. Yours is to inhabit your future; to dare to make a difference and to dare to matter. Life is good and you will be as happy as you want to be if you can learn to visit the core of your sorrow and still see the berries. In 1946, those who loved me rejoiced at my birth. Do the same for me now. Rejoice at my rebirth into the eternal.

Amo, amas, amat

Epilogue

Dear Girls,

Amid the controversy surrounding today's anniversary of Columbus's discovery and his treatment of the Indians, this log has helped me discover that he and I have much in common. Columbus set out unsure of where he was going, wasn't sure how to get there, didn't know how far it was, and didn't know how long it would take. Upon arrival, he didn't know where he really was or how far he'd come. After returning home he didn't know where he'd been or that he hadn't gone where he wanted to go. That's how I often felt about this undertaking. However, this log is also a glimpse into my private life-album at people and places I've loved; a sharing of the sacredness of my journey. In years to come, when my memories have no human home, this *adversaria* will remember them for me. These pages, serving as both windows and doorknobs, will allow you to visit who I was back when I was.

I'm confident I could have survived in this world on my own. I could have grown strong and independent on my own. I could have educated myself, prepared myself, supported myself, and achieved some measure of financial success on my own. What I could not have done on my own was to have become human. This log is full of pages full of words; my search with a pen for places where I could begin again. I know it doesn't answer all your questions or any of them completely. It wasn't designed to. The questions were mine and thus so are the answers. However, I hope it helped to generate questions within you, leading to more questions that lead to still more questions, each helping you to determine what else is to be learned. And if you learned one-tenth as much from reading this as I learned from writing it, then I learned ten times more than you did.

The Latin term "carpe diem" summarizes my current favorite philosophy. Literally translated, it means, "Seize the day." First used by the Roman poet Horace over two thousand years ago, the complete expression was *"Carpe diem, quam minimum credula postero."* and means "Enjoy today, trusting little in tomorrow." Although it was once used to encourage women to give up their virginity, carpe diem isn't an excuse for doing anything we want. Rather, it's a battle cry for those wishing to break free of their chains to experience the joys life offers. It speaks to those failing to reach their potential because they worry about what others will think, how they'll look if they'll fail, or any number of excuses that drain the vitality and wonder from their lives. Like carpe diem, real living isn't about the abandonment of morality, but rather about the joy of abandoning life in the harbor.

Author Your Life,

Dad

CPSIA information can be obtained
at www.ICGtesting.com
Printed in the USA
BVHW041005240122
627011BV00016B/815